Agnes Elizabeth

Gracious Living

ALSO BY ADELE WILLIAMS

Thrift Shop Decorating

Gracious Living

How to Enjoy Being a Woman

by ADELE WILLIAMS

ARBOR HOUSE
New York

COPYRIGHT © 1976 BY ADELE WILLIAMS

ALL RIGHTS RESERVED, INCLUDING THE RIGHT OF REPRODUCTION IN WHOLE OR IN PART IN ANY FORM. PUBLISHED IN THE UNITED STATES BY ARBOR HOUSE PUBLISHING COMPANY, INC. AND IN CANADA BY CLARKE, IRWIN & COMPANY, LTD.

LIBRARY OF CONGRESS CATALOGUE CARD NUMBER: 76-029227

ISBN: 0-87795-149-7

Contents

Introduction vii

PART ONE: A BETTER WAY

CHAPTER 1 Climbing Out of the Dreary Job 3
CHAPTER 2 Looking Great 11
CHAPTER 3 Design for Living 22
CHAPTER 4 Entertaining in Style 30
CHAPTER 5 Keys to Success: Your Manners and Speech 38
CHAPTER 6 Starting Your Own Business 42
CHAPTER 7 Making It, Keeping It, Enjoying It 48
CHAPTER 8 Escaping from the "American Dream," Including the Chrome-plated Nightmare 53
CHAPTER 9 Liberate Yourself from Consumer Brainwashing 59
CHAPTER 10 Stop Cluttering Your Life with Gadgets 72
CHAPTER 11 Are We Becoming a Nation of Slobs? 76
CHAPTER 12 An Elegant House: Order, Simplicity, Color 81
CHAPTER 13 Thoughts on Keeping House 87
CHAPTER 14 Liberation: Having the Best in the Best of All Possible Worlds 95

Contents

PART TWO: COMING OF AGE

CHAPTER 15 *The Freedom to Be Yourself* 107

CHAPTER 16 *Setting the Stage for a New Life: Your Clothes, Your Looks, Your House* 114

CHAPTER 17 *Money: Saving It, Making More* 120

CHAPTER 18 *Man Talk* 128

CHAPTER 19 *Europe on Nothing a Day* 135

CHAPTER 20 *Husband-hunting? Relax and Enjoy It* 139

CHAPTER 21 *You're Old Enough to Know Better* 143

CHAPTER 22 *Menus and Recipes* 147

Introduction

Success—It's All Yours If You Want It

Once, not too long ago, I owned a shop in Palm Beach, a very expensive little luxury shop—antiques, flower arrangements, table linens. I was right next door to Elizabeth Arden, and my customers were the happiest women I ever met. Liberated? They were liberated all right, liberated from premature old age, from drudgery, from boredom, from ugliness, from worry and anxiety—they were just about the most liberated women I ever met.

I tried to analyze why they seemed so supremely happy. It was not simply that they were rich; most were but some were not. I had met hundreds of miserable rich women during my checkered career in fashion, cosmetics, and decorating; money alone was not the reason.

These women, I finally realized, had learned how to live

successfully as women. Young or not so young, some frankly old; single, married, and widowed—they ran the gamut from a successful decorator and famous author, the thirtyish wife of a seventy-year-old millionaire (incidentally one of the best-looking men in town), to a seventy-five-year-old *grande dame* who gave the best parties in Palm Beach and whose favorite evening dress was a long-sleeved black sequin sheath that clung to every inch of her size ten figure.

They looked great, and they loved clothes, flowers, pretty things for the house—all the things women used to be encouraged to like. Superficial? Not really. They created happiness around them, for they had learned at some point in their lives—or maybe they were just born with the knowledge—that a woman can have anything she wants if she knows how to get it, and that the way to get it is not through militant assertiveness but with that old fashioned word "charm," and that almost forgotten quality, elegance.

And they *were* charming, and fun to have as clients. They made me feel happier; they were enthusiastic and knowledgeable, and they had style, flair, and a natural, unpretentious elegance.

The more I thought about it, the more I realized that the reason I had enjoyed my shop in New York and now in Palm Beach so much was that most of my customers were so pleasant. I did occasionally have someone who was anxious, uptight and defensive, but it seemed that most women who were interested in flowered table linens, ruffled pillows, and baskets of flowers—my stock in trade —were enjoying life as women.

To me, the women's liberation movement is incredibly

depressing. The fact is, there *are* all too many women who live lives of drab frustration, trapped by dull jobs at low pay or by the day-in, day-out drudgery of rearing children and keeping house. They are inwardly enraged at the meanness of their lot. But the women's liberation movement is a protest, however valid, in the wrong direction.

During the past fifty years two forces have driven most women into the deadly trap in which they now find themselves. The first, the demand for women's rights such as the right to vote and the opportunity to enter the working world, led to genuine improvement; but the "opportunity" quickly became a trap. Untrained, eager women accepted almost any job just to have a chance. As a result, they were quickly absorbed as a source of cheap labor. The routine, the boring, the dead-end jobs went to women—"they're going to leave in a few short years and marry, so why train them for something better?" That was the reasoning then and in large measure that's the reasoning today. Unfortunately, it has an element of truth.

Women do fall in love, marry, and have children, and unless they desperately need the money or the job is an interesting, lucrative one, they often leave it, only to fall into what I call trap number two: The American Dream.

The rapid advance in technology has brought us a cornucopia of products (or is it a Pandora's Box?) designed to make life easier, more entertaining, or more interesting—at least, that's what the manufacturers tell us. Actually, they are primarily designed to make a profit, and that's not evil either, if—and this is the big "if"—we exercise our God-given *right of choice*.

Unfortunately, we have largely forgotten we *have* a

choice, we have been so thoroughly brainwashed into believing that the good life is a suburban house, containing all the "work-saving" apparatus that time payments can be stretched to meet. A car—that ultimate American toy—is never even considered as a choice; you *must* have a car. And now of course you must have not one but several television sets, at least one in color, so that you may absorb even more hard sell. There is rarely any money left over for what are generally regarded as luxuries.

Little wonder the woman who has become a slave to her "work-saving" appliances and the endless truckman's job of chauffeuring is hardly a happy, charming companion. But let's put in a word of pity for the male half of the house. No job is all play, and any even somewhat demanding job is fraught with tension; add to this the nightly encounter with screaming children, shrewish wife, and blaring television set, and it's small wonder the guy holds a job at all.

But what's to be done? Demand that the man assume half of the housework and the care of the children? Campaign for equality with men, for the right to do a man's job at a man's pay? Who are we kidding? I shall always remember the *New Yorker* cartoon depicting two overall-clad Russian women in construction helmets laboring with pickaxes in a drainage ditch. One was saying to the other, "Well, you can't say we are not ahead of the United States in women's liberation." Thanks, but no thanks, and I don't think I'm alone. In my opinion—and I'm very opinionated—what women really want is to be free of the slavery they have eagerly entered into of their own volition—and girls, a pickaxe is not going to set you free.

Introduction

What *is* going to set you free is a willingness to succeed as a woman, whether in a career or a marriage or both; to try to stop competing with men and start to learn or renew what I hope you instinctively know: that charm, an aura of happiness, and an element of wit, coupled with a dash of elegance, is going to get you further, and do it faster and more pleasurably, than all the legislation that politicians can muster.

No, this is not a servile bowing to male chauvinism; the truth is, successful men are charming, too. What about Jack Kennedy, Cary Grant, Franklin Roosevelt, Adlai Stevenson, John Lindsay? They and every other successful man I know of could charm the birds out of the trees. I've never met a single dreary success, male *or* female, and I don't believe they exist.

Assuming you go along with me (and I presume you will at least a bit longer), the problem is how? How can you escape the dreary job, cope with the children–housework syndrome–end the boredom of lonely middle or old age? You can, you know, and without a lot of time or money. You do need the determination to change your life and the courage to break with old habits and preconceived ideas, but that's all you need—and it's all yours if you want it.

PART ONE
A Better Way

Chapter One

Climbing Out of the Dreary Job

*I*f you are stuck with a boring job that pays enough to get by but not enough to make life pleasant, get out of it. The first thing to do is to evaluate the job and whom you are working for. If you are low woman in the typing pool for Amalgamated Wire Twisters Inc., and you're not particularly keen on wire twisters, then you need another job. Maybe it will be just as low end, but if there's something to move up to you can probably climb the mountain. Now I'm going to say something that will send the feminists screaming to their banners, but it's rule one if what you want is success without beating your brains out: *It is easier to succeed in a woman-oriented field.* Oh dear, now I've said it, *but I'm not sorry.* Dedicated scientists and calculus experts aside, you'll have a better chance of moving to the top if you can add the asset—yes, asset—of your femininity to your other abilities.

Retailing, decorating, advertising, cosmetics, food, home furnishings, architecture, journalism, real estate, fashion design and promotion, editing and publishing are all fields that women can excel in—*easily*. This is not to say that a woman can't be just as good a lawyer, engineer, or building contractor as a man, but it's *harder*; and if what you want is the pleasure of success, why do it the hard way?

Long before anyone thought of women's lib, women were carving out spectacular careers for themselves in fields particularly adapted to them. Dorothy Shaver, president of Lord & Taylor; Ruby Ross Woods, one of the world's highest paid decorators; Oveta Culp Hobby, publisher of the Houston *Post*, Elizabeth Arden; Madame Helena Rubenstein; Ida Bailey Allen; Coco Chanel (one of the most alluring women who ever lived); Dorothy Draper, the woman who decorated the famous Greenbrier resort; Carmel Snow, editor of *Harper's Bazaar*; Edna Wollman Chase, editor of *Vogue*, are only a few of the women who reached the pinnacle of success back in the thirties. Today, you need only look around you—the really successful women are in women-oriented fields: Estée Lauder; Mary Wells, president of Wells, Rich & Green, one of the top advertising agencies in the country; Gerry Stutz, president of Bendel's, that ultra chic New York specialty shop; Mabel Julianelli, president of Julianelli shoes... The list could go on endlessly, and believe me, you can be very sure that not one of these ladies made it by attending street rallies clad in a parka and wool stockings.

Climbing Out of the Dreary Job 5

Where to start? Begin simply by deciding what appeals to you most. Are you terribly interested in how your house looks? Do furniture, antiques, curtains and rugs "turn you on"? Or are you a serious book hound, never happier than when you can be left alone with a book? Maybe clothes are your great interest and you like nothing better than putting a wardrobe together. Remember the woman whose idea of heaven was to be naked in Bergdorf's with a checkbook? Only you can decide what vocation really appeals to you; once you've decided, go shopping for a job in that field and that field only. Take a smaller salary if you must, but don't even waste time on interviews with Associated Iron Works when what you really want is to decorate houses or run a flower shop. Yes, I know it's easy to say go get a job in the field you prefer, but what if you lack even the barest essentials of training for the work you want to do? The answer is simple, but like most simple answers it is hard to put into practice: be willing to start at the bottom—not reluctantly and grudgingly, but enthusiastically.

Let me tell you one hard fact: no business ever has enough good Indians: Chiefs are a dime a dozen, but Indians? Good ones are as rare as plovers' eggs. Retail stores across the country are pleading for good saleswomen, you can pick and choose; competent typists and secretaries can get into any business they like—and if being a saleswoman in a department store or specialty shop or a typist in a decorator's office or on a magazine sounds like the end of no place, think again. There is no better place to learn merchandising than on the selling floor, no better way to learn the hard business facts about decorating, publishing, or what have you than working in the office of someone who has made it. The beautiful part is that you will have almost no competition if you are really determined to climb the success ladder. The sheer incompetence, indifference, and sometimes plain old stupidity of the average employee is all in your favor. Just ordinary enthusiasm, willingness, and dependability will set you apart so fast that the "powers" will immediately mark you as someone to watch.

Above all, don't be a job snob. It doesn't matter in the least if you have a college degree or have spent four years in design school; what you want is a chance in a profession of your choice, and if getting a foothold in that profession means taking a low-end job, it doesn't matter; if you really love what you are doing you can't help rising faster than bubbles in a glass of champagne.

The secret is still that tired old advice to would-be executives: be willing—no, more than willing, *avid* to learn. Don't just do the work that's put in front of you; find out *what* makes a particular dress sell, *why* the editor selected that particular article, the *reason* the decorator decided on that fabric or piece of furniture. "Why?" is perhaps the most important word in business language. Of course all this doesn't mean a damn thing if what you really want is to join the great unwashed and live in a commune. I know it's unfashionable to take the Horatio Alger approach, but if you, like me, would rather dine on a good steak than hot dogs, and if you like the silky feel of good clothes and prefer a nice hot bath with plenty of bath salts and lots of luxurious towels to a cold shower, then you had better get on with making money—because, honey, there is simply no way to have all the pleasant things in this world without cash. So unless your family

Climbing Out of the Dreary Job

left you a trust fund or you marry a rich man, the only way to get it is to be successful. Failures simply aren't paid very much.

Assuming you would prefer success, where do we go from here? Charles Revson, the man who started making nail polish in his mother's garage and built it into the Revlon cosmetics empire, said the one single most important key to success was sheer, dogged, won't-give-up determination, that it meant more than brains, talent, or education. He was probably right; what he meant was a hell-fire, gutsy will to succeed, and since so many people have made up their minds that they won't make it (yes, they have, just look around you), determination is undoubtedly the elusive key. And I'd like to add another factor that has paid off for me and for most of the successful people I know, and that is plain old unglamorous dependability. If that sounds dreary, let me assure you that if people find out you can be depended upon, their kingdom is yours. We all know the secretary who couldn't finish the letters on time (her mother called), the girl that didn't show up the day the store was having a big sale (*her* mother *didn't* call), the assistant fashion coordinator who forgot the shoes (*she* called her mother). Then there is the all-too-frequent bearer of bad news: she can't come to work because her husband can't start the car, the bus has broken down, the plumbing has gone afoul, her stove caught fire, etc., etc., etc. Finally, we have Typhoid Mary. She has every illness that's going around: in March it's a cold, in April the flu, in May a sprained ankle, in June she has been bitten by a wasp, in July it's a painful sunburn, and so on up through frostbite in December. When she does show up for work, she has an assortment of aspirin bottles, mouthwashes and prescription containers conspicuously displayed on her desk. Short periods of work are interrupted by endless sessions in the ladies' room, and when the long day draws to a close (it has seemed very, very long to her employer) she leaves early, with the cheerful farewell, "I'm still not feeling too well—I guess I'd better go home and go to bed." Employers have been known to sit staring into space for hours after her departure.

The sheer absence of such performances will set you apart from the crowd. Simply having the letters ready for the mail boy, showing up cheerfully *on time*, leaving your troubles at home, and making an effort to stay attractively well and healthy (if you are really sick, shut up and go home) will make you a star performer in any business. And last but not least—For God's Sake Keep Your Mouth Firmly Shut on the Subject of Female Disorders.

There's still another quality that in my opinion is absolutely essential for rising to the top, and lack of it has probably held back more good people than any other single factor: the ability to "take it." Any creative field, and all of the fields I have mentioned demand some degree of creativity, are fraught with tension, and the successful people in them are usually high-key performers who drive themselves and their employees relentlessly. They think nothing of working until seven at night and taking work home over the weekend, and they expect their key people to do the same. Success is not a nine to five operation. Of course there are some creative employers who have a calm, orderly way of operating, but not many, so if you care more about coffee breaks and leaving on time, think twice before you leave Amalgamated Wire Twisters.

Another point to consider is the fact that creative people often have low boiling points. If criticism, whether justified or not, sends you weeping to the ladies' room, then by all means remain with A.W.T.

On the other hand, if you're tough enough to take it, then here's a word of advice that will put you in the tax bracket you prefer almost before you start. Try to find a job in a relatively small organization where you will work with the top people and where the boss is known to be both difficult and demanding. No one else has been able to handle the situation, and here you are, with a cool eye and a steady grip on the wheel; my dear, they will give you anything your little heart desires. I know; I was the latest in succession of nine promotion directors in two years when I joined Elizabeth Arden. Everyone said I was crazy to leave my safe but somewhat dull job. Miss Arden was famous for her temper, and she had a delightful habit of *arriving* at the office at five p.m. That was the only time you could see her to get an okay on anything, and *nothing*, not even a letter, went out without her okay. How long did I last? Eleven of the happiest years of my life, and I left only because I was offered an increase in salary so large I couldn't resist it. I still regret it; Elizabeth Arden was more fun. My rewards came in tangible ways: a generous salary, trips to Europe, lavish presents (I still have the 18-carat gold Tiffany bracelet), and fond memories of the lovely clothes, lingerie, cosmetics, and perfume. My intangible reward came in the form of devotion to a ruthless perfectionist who taught me to be one too.

Jobs become careers because of what you put into them, but that "What" has got to be a lot more than simply getting to work and doing what you are asked to do. You've got to get involved, you've got to care about the business; it has to be important to you that the magazine is great, or the black lace promotion is a hit, or the book is a bestseller, or the redecorated town house is just what the client wanted. Only then can you make your mark, because, though this simple fact seems to have escaped many employees' notice, most businesses are run with the intention of making a profit. You can expect to be rewarded in direct ratio to the amount you contribute to this elementary aim.

So much for some basic truths. Tiresome as they may be to hear, they are nonetheless like the foundation to a house: without them the whole thing is going to collapse.

Chapter Two

Looking Great

*L*et's assume you have landed a job in the field you want, that you are learning fast, and that you are both determined and dependable. Now how do you lift yourself out of the ordinary, make yourself into something "special"? You do it with one word—"style"—and it's a lot easier than you think. Style is the way you look, the way you sound, the way you act, and the impact you make. To develop a style of your own, start with your looks. First, stop paying any attention at all to most fashion magazines. Really chic women do not slavishly follow their advertising, or even most of the editorials, both of which are largely designed to sell merchandise, particularly cosmetics.

Now, how can I say this so that I won't hurt anyone's feelings? Oh, to hell with it—I'll just say it: most women are divided into one of two types. The first, usually young, is very preoccupied with her looks; her hair is frequently too long and/or combed in a far too elaborate style, her eyelids are lavishly coated with green, purple, or blue shadow, and she makes generous use of eyeliners, foundations, and lipstick, all in "this year's colors." If short skirts are "in," hers are the shortest on record, but she won't give up her high heels to balance the brief skirt line. She wears the tightest of pants whatever the size of her rear, and of course she goes in heavily for costume jewelry and not too good perfume.

At the other end of the scale we have Mrs. Dowdy, who has mentally given up and has decided to be "comfortable." Her favorite costume is the knit pants suit in relentless colors that she fancies will be bright and cheery. These costumes (which should be outlawed), worn for everything but weddings and funerals, make her look as wide as a barn, the too-short jacket that cuts across the fanny effectively making her look even wider.

These ladies don't go in for makeup, except for a little lipstick, of course, which, since their skin has withered from neglect, usually has an unfortunate tendency to creep into the wrinkles around their mouths. Naturally, they don't wear perfume. The final sin is their choice of shoes, which are bought for comfort, are all too often white, and have the devastating result of making their feet look monstrously huge.

Now that I have been as unpleasant as possible (and I hasten to add there are loads of exceptions to these categories), what can any woman do to look really chic, to develop a style of her own? Through an accident of fate and fortune I have been thrown in with some of the chicest women in the world, and have had the opportunity of observing them at close hand. Here are a few key points followed like a religion by the beautiful people that will unfailingly result in a better looking you.

#1. You are what you eat. Resolve as of today to change your eating habits, if necessary, to a diet that is almost completely made up of fresh fruit and vegetables, cheese, lean meat, fish, and liver or other organ meats like sweetbreads. If you drink, hold it down to one or two cocktails a day—try wine with meals instead. Cut out candy, soft drinks, potato chips—all "junk" food. Believe me, the really elegant girls of this world are very, very careful about what they eat. They know only too well that really good skin, a trim figure, glossy hair and a total absence of unpleasant and dreary minor illnesses are due almost entirely to what's on the menu.

#2. Don't have colds. Colds are tacky and unnecessary; get enough vitamin C to avoid them. (See diet above.)

#3. Get your teeth fixed even if you have to sell the furniture to pay for it. Go to the trouble of finding a top-flight dentist, and work with him until your teeth are in the best possible shape. Chic people do not have bad teeth.

#4. Get a really good haircut for a super-simple style. A gleaming straight cut or a sleeked-back knot is far more chic than any complicated, fussy "do." If your hair is gray and wispy, don't ever have it set in tight curls—try to get it in shape (see diet above), and give it a few treatments for gloss. Dye if you must, but unless you are awfully talented it's better to have it done either professionally or not at all. Contrary to what the ads say, homemade dye jobs usually look just that, homemade. Whatever you do, don't go too far afield from what nature intended; if you are a dark brunette you are only going to look like a freak as a platinum blonde.

#5. Now about clothes. Few women look their best in pants. All the liberation in the world will not change the fact that nature gave women smaller waists and bigger hips than men, and unless you really have a small backside and narrow hips you are not doing yourself any favor in pants. If you insist on wearing them anyway, pick neutral colors like beige, gray, navy blue, or brown (white is okay for resorts if you are thin), and make sure they are made of a fairly substantial fabric like poplin, gabardine, or flannel—never never knits. The elegant girls who do wear pants stick to these rules. Also, never even try on pants suits. Jersey tops, sweaters, and shirts are the only toppings for pants.

Unless you have money to burn, don't buy brightly colored clothes; in fact, don't buy them anyway. The late, great Norman Norell loved beige—he said it was any woman's best color. And beware of prints; most prints, unless they are fabulously expensive, are hideous.

Economize if you must on a dress or a skirt, but treat yourself to really elegant shoes. Shoes are a dead giveaway. You can get by with a ten-dollar denim dress you have made yourself if your shoes are right. Unfortunately they run into money, but they last indefinitely if properly care for. I don't own a pair of shoes less than two years old. The best, in my opinion, are made by Mario of Florence (General Motors Plaza, New York), Helene Arpels (665 Madison Avenue, New York) and Gucci (New York and Palm Beach), the last especially for shoes to wear with pants. Wear tennis shoes or espadrilles around the house, but treat yourself to really good shoes for your public appearances. If one pair is all you can afford, buy black patent. Yes, you can wear patent in winter, and black goes with any neutral color.

The same goes for handbags: save up for one by Gucci or Hermès (Bonwit Teller, New York). Buy it on the installment plan if you have to (I did), and take care of it. I have a black Hermès bag, painfully paid for over a ten-month period, that I have been using with pleasure for *nineteen* years! Believe me, a good bag and good shoes set you apart immediately with people who know, and they are who count in the success world.

Good bags and shoes, I know, are a little difficult to pay for if you are just starting to climb; but if you cut back on other clothes, and especially if you can sew your own, they can usually be managed. Actually, three simple skirts or dresses will get you by. Try saving in small ways, too, like bringing your lunch to work. Not a dreary sandwich, though; make it some good cheese and fruit (that's style, too). Your boss may ask to join you.

Train your eye to see what really looks good on you. Most women are flattered by an A-line skirt, and unless you have really narrow hips it's usually a mistake to wear an absolutely straight line—still another reason why pants are an unfortunate choice. I know they are comfortable (so is a bathrobe), and "everybody wears them," but that's just why you shouldn't. You are out to set a style of your own, remember? How can you, if you wear what everyone else wears?

Let's try to do the impossible and dream up a perfect small wardrobe for the girl (no matter what her age) who is long on ambition but short on cash.

FALL THROUGH SPRING

Three very simple wrap A-line skirts: one beige, one camel color, one black. These are easy to make even for beginner seamstresses.

Six tops: a black V-neck sweater with long sleeves; two beige jersey pullovers, one with a turtle neck; two or three shirts. These unfortunately run into money, but a really well-tailored, long-sleeved shirt can be very chic indeed. If you can make your own you can have luxurious shirts for peanuts.

Now you are going to need a couple of good belts, one beige, one black. Look for the belts designed by Mimi D'N. You buy one set of good-looking buckles and add the leather part in the colors you want.

If you can afford only one coat and winters are cold in your part of the country, a classic beige poplin raincoat, fur-lined if possible, will give you the most "looks" for your money.

Be super-careful when it comes to costume jewelry. By that I *don't* mean sticking to that dreary little strand of "pearls" and itsy-bitsy earrings, but your costume jewelry should have snap; it should make a statement. Never wear "dainty" rings. If you wear a ring at all, it should be a chunky one. For a little guidance in jewelry shopping, try to get to Tiffany's in New York or one of their other locations (Houston, San Francisco, Atlanta, Beverly Hills, Chicago). Study their designs and then look for "knock offs" at costume jewelry counters—the exciting pieces are copied within weeks. (Of course, as soon as you hit the money just go to Tiffany's.) Another favorite jeweler of the super-chic is David Webb. I have personally never had the nerve to go browsing at David Webb's 7 East Fifty-seventh Street boutique, but I do shop the windows, and it's pretty enticing. Needless to say, these little bijoux are quickly copied, too, and with a discerning eye you can make some pretty good choices.

As for other accessories, you are going to need a couple of good scarves (practice tying them until they look right). I like the imported cotton ones best—Neiman-Marcus (Dallas, Atlanta, Miami, St. Louis, and Houston) imports some from Fisba Staffels that are great. The colors and prints are so good you can just tell them to choose a couple for you, you can't miss. You'll also want gloves—plain, heavy English cotton doeskin will do, but it's nice to have one pair in beige leather lined in silk for warmth and that luxurious feeling. We've already discussed shoes and bags, so we can go on to stockings. Get the palest ones you can find. *Never* wear black stockings.

Now all this may sound pretty tame, but it's an elegant, chic little wardrobe. You can always add to it, but don't tart it up. Believe me, you will look so different from your fellowworkers in their Easter egg-tinted pants suits and their sleazy over-done dresses, people will stop on the street to look at you.

Add to these essentials a couple of long evening skirts. Make sure one is black—it will look great with your black sweater. If you want to give it real dash, write to Cepelia (63 East 57 St., New York) for a couple of their copies of Elsa Perretti's "diamonds by the yard." These are fine chains, designed for Tiffany's, that resemble "gold" twine set at intervals with tiny "diamonds." Pretty smashing.

For summer it's easy enough to shift the pattern to

linen and cotton, particularly denim. Try making one of the colors pale blue denim—it looks great with a tan—or change to a good-looking shirt-dress with a low V neckline.

Hats are a bore with winter wardrobes, unless you have the kind of super good looks that can get away with a knit cap pulled down over your ears. This is okay on a snowy day; otherwise wear scarves, *not* tied under your chin. But in hot weather nothing looks better than a wide-brimmed straw hat—not the floppy garden party variety, but a planter's hat, plain and elegant, and if it costs more than $6 don't buy it, it will be jazzed up too much.

Now for a few opinionated opinions on makeup. The best advice is no advice—don't wear it. Very few chic women wear any at all these days; it's been over-done. Lipstick, if you must, but a clear gel that gives just a little color is better, and if you have pale or scanty lashes a little brown mascara is okay, but that's it. Chic women have great skins, glowing not with "Liquid Luster Living Foundation" but with health, the result of an intelligent diet plus exercise, exercise, exercise. Yes, I know it's fun to slather goo on your face, and watching what you eat and keeping your circulation surging around sounds like pretty tiresome advice, but it's the only way, and once you get started, you'll find that exercise can be addictive. As for creams and lotions that are supposed to keep you looking nineteen forever, the answer is very simple, **they won't**. You can't put moisture in your skin from the outside, and wrinkles are caused more by poor circulation and bad diet than by age. They appear, inevitably it seems to most women, as the cumulative result of years of bad food—low in protein, vitamins and minerals—plus growing inactivity as the years tick off. All you really need on your skin for occasional surface dryness (the only kind that can be corrected externally) is a little grease or oil, and petroleum jelly will do as good a job as anything. This is God's truth, and I know; I spent eleven years of my life as a cosmetics executive. The truth was, Elizabeth Arden herself exercised every day of her life, swam frequently, didn't smoke, was an absolute fanatic about bad food and what she called "garbage" (soft drinks, snacks, candy, etc.), and she drank only an occasional cocktail. These are the principles she put into practice when she opened her now-famous "Maine Chance" and they remain the same today. As a matter of fact, it was Gaylord Hauser, the health food pioneer, who developed the original menus for Maine Chance, and they have changed very little.

Use the money you have been spending on cosmetics to join a health club and let the sauna, whirlpool bath, and swimming pool give you the glow you want. And while you are about it, bone up on nutrition—Gaylord Hauser's books are available in paperback for a couple of dollars (incidentally, he's eighty-four at this writing and looks no more than fifty).

Now I will climb off my soapbox and move on to a list of cardinal sins that I hope you will not commit. I admit to having committed most of them myself years ago before I found out how awful they were, and having paid dearly for my rashness will endeavor to save you from a similar fate. It's harder to undo a bad impression than to create a good one, so here goes.

Don't go to extremes of fashion. If skirts are short, you don't have to wear the shortest one on record. If they are long, that doesn't mean you have to get yourself up as Whistler's mother.

Never wear matching accessories. Even if both handbag and shoes are black, have the shoes in patent and the bag in leather. Nothing is more horrendous than matching shoes and handbags.

Never wear matched sets of jewelry—I don't care if they are matching diamonds. The only permissible matching jewelry is a pair of earrings.

Avoid wearing flowers at any cost, no matter whose feelings get hurt. It's time he learned.

Never wear pants that cup under the fanny, I beg of you. Look at your backside in the mirror; pants that cling to the bottom are not sexy, just tacky.

Please don't wear "summer jewelry," those awful things of white enamel and gilt, or even worse, flower pins, like big enameled daisies—God forbid; The same is true for those dreadful "jeweled" Christmas trees, or any other seasonal decoration. You are not the public library.

There are times when boots are a necessity—in the rain or snow—but may providence protect you if you are foolish enough to appear in boots with anything but storm gear. As for white or colored plastic boots, it pains me even to mention them here. Get some elegant plain black boots and wear them when, and only when, the weather calls for them.

I don't think I'll ever recover from the sight of a pretty

little southern girl tripping down the street one July afternoon in a skirt that barely covered her bottom and a pair of thigh-high white plastic boots. I thought it was the shimmering heat that made me sick. It wasn't.

I've already touched on makeup, however, if you insist on wearing it please, lay off the blue, purple, green or metallic eye shadows. They just are *not* worn. Nor is nail polish—buff your nails to a satiny sheen instead.

Avoid "dainty," "feminine" clothes—lace-trimmed blouses, embroidered sweaters, crocheted shawls or stoles, embroidered handkerchiefs, in fact embroidered anything. And the older you are the more strenuously you should avoid them.

I've already mentioned stockings, but what about textured ones? They're great with the right shoes for a country or casual look. Beige is still the best color, and while black is still awful (it makes you look as if you are going to a street rally), it's not too bad to venture into other neutral colors, but don't wear textured stockings with city slicker shoes—ever.

Finally, so-called sexy clothes are not sexy, just pathetic. You can be sure the only reaction you'll get from men, whether you know it or not, is patronizing amusement. Oh, sure, the sliding neckline, the transparent blouse, the vampy shoe may get you an invitation to hop into bed—why not? You are obviously available, and it's free, isn't it? But amusement is still the prime emotional response, so if you *like* to be laughed at, go ahead.

Chapter Three

Design for Living

Now what? You have the job, all is going well, you are the picture of understated chic, but there is still work to be done. You are going to have to create an image, and that means a background for yourself, and *that* means where and how you live.

Before we go into details on how to make your background contribute to your success, I'd like to make one point abundantly clear. Do *not* have a roommate, male or female. Oh, yes, I know it's a brave new world and lots of men and women room together and *everybody* thinks it's just grand. Well, dear, it's not, it's simply tacky. Have all the affairs you want—they are none of my business; have an affair openly if it makes you happy, though it is a bit limiting, but make sure he has his place and you have yours. Why? Because it's simply middle-class ordinary to have a roommate, regardless of sex. Now if that sounds like pretentious affectation, well, I can only tell you that if you are going to lift yourself out of the dreary rut too many women find themselves in you can't do, wear, say, or eat what's ordinary—and that's simply telling you like it is, not affectation.

Now *where* are you going to live? First, of all, strive mightily to avoid living in the suburbs. I know this may be difficult if you are married and have small children and a mortgage, or living with your widowed mother and mummy won't give up the old homestead, or if both mummy and daddy are clinging to the O.H., but stay out of the suburbs if you possibly can.

What's wrong with the suburbs? Again, it is the ordinary thing to do. (I'm going to get piles of nasty letters on this one, but I'm hell bent on writing the truth as I know it, not simply rehashing pretty little platitudes.) A few other things wrong with the suburbs: first, you simply cannot be as chic and well groomed as you have to be if you are forced to take a long train or bus ride twice a day (or worse yet, a grinding drive through rush-hour traffic). Second, you are undoubtedly going to be late for work more often than success allows, and finally, that pleasant custom of asking someone important to you to stop by for a drink after work is obviously impossible.

What's to be done about it? If the marriage-mortgage-children situation is the problem, be ruthless; sell the house and move into town. Drastic? Of course, and your husband will undoubtedly think you have lost your mind, but if you can talk it over calmly he will probably like the idea. After all, he's not exactly having fun commuting either, and the two of you just might enjoy being able to stash the kids with a babysitter and go out to dinner at a good restaurant. The truth is, a very great many men are secretly (or openly) a bit fed up with family-room fun and those jolly cook-outs.

And cities are great places for kids. There are parks, libraries, museums, and zoos, and most important, good private schools, the only schools you *can afford*. Yes, here's that pretentious snobbery rearing its ugly head again, but it's still another reason why you had better be a success. Yes, I know, you can hardly send your children to private school on a salesgirl's salary, but you can use part of the proceeds of the sale of your house and car (yes, car) to finance the tuition until you can get going.

Now I've managed to sneak it in—selling your car is probably the best move you can make. You don't need one in town; public transportation and taxis are generally available, and it's often a lot more fun to walk. Cities are great for walking. If you do take the plunge and sell the car, you will not only get rid of one big monthly payment but you also eliminate insurance, repairs, and gasoline, all of which take a hefty bite out of anyone's income. If you insist on driving to God knows where on a weekend you can always rent a car for not too much money.

Let's see now, we have most of you married girls taken care of. Isn't that really boring conceit on my part? Yes, it is, but from my vantage point of more than forty years of observing the girls who made it and the girls who didn't, the odds are heavily in your favor if you do as I tell you.

However, let's assume that some of you have mother to contend with. And let's get morbid and assume that neither of you has enough money to live separately, and that your mother bursts into tears at the thought of leaving her house. Furthermore, you can't bring yourself to leave her alone. Again, you have to be ruthless: sell the house and move into town anyway. You may have a tough time convincing your mother, but you can probably bring her around to your way of thinking if you tell her your career is at stake and you *need* her help and cooperation. One very effective way to persuade her is to bring her into the city for a one- or two-day stay. Get her to have her hair done at the best salon in town, spend an hour or two shopping, and wind up the festivities with dinner in an interesting restaurant. She may begin to think Tupperware parties are not so much fun after all, and the Avon lady is a bit of a bore. One way or another, though, you've got to sell her on the move. Once she's settled, try to get her interested in some activity—a course at a museum, learning a foreign language—or buy her a small dog; anything to avoid the tearful scenes about how much she misses her house and all of her friends. You can't afford to be upset and still keep your mind on the job. This is all going to take money, of course, but like your married counterpart, you can use part of the proceeds from your house to finance the move.

If all else fails, get your mother to rent her house for a year and *try* living in the city. This will probably go down easier; after all, it's only temporary, or at least will seem so. When the year is up she may refuse to leave the city and will gladly sell the house, or happily you may be earning enough money to make it on your own and your mother can return to suburbia. Meanwhile, the savings from commuting expense can pay for your mother's movies or adult education or whatever.

Mummy-plus-daddy offers a real problem. Somehow, men do not adjust as readily to change as women, and if daddy is retired it's even worse. He will probably hate the city, and you will all be miserable. After all, he can't go and have *his* hair done—unisex hairdressers simply haven't caught on with his generation (which is also mine). In that case, there is only one thing to do: leave. Unless your financial contribution is an absolute necessity, strike out on your own. Your parents have each other, after all. As painful as it may be, take off and find yourself an apartment on your own, even if it's nothing more than one room on the fourth floor of a walk-up building. One word of caution, however; don't move into a questionable neighborhood. Settle for less apartment, cut down on everything else, but you must have a "good" address. Besides, it's playing with fire to live in a bad area. No, it is not quaint or resourceful, it's just not very bright.

Married or single, mother along or alone, try to find an apartment in an older building. If it's well kept, the high ceilings and spacious rooms (often with a fireplace) more than offset the lack of built-in conditioning and gadgety kitchens. And an older building is more likely to have larger apartments, vital if you have a family or if your mother is living with you; you need a minimum of two bedrooms.

Since I don't know where you live I can only generalize and I am sure you think I have a lot of nerve blithely telling you to sell your house or your family's house. It may not be economically feasible, but I do say if you move into an area where you are not dependent on a car for transportation and can get to work easily, you are going to find life a lot easier and pleasanter. What's more you are going to have a better chance of success. Wherever there are suburbs there are bound to be cities, large or not so large, and attractive living quarters are to be found in what is sometimes referred to as the "inner city." In fact, in hundreds of cities across the country old neighborhoods are being rediscovered, and the still handsome town houses and older apartment buildings are being renovated or restored. You couldn't do better than to get in on the ground floor, either by buying or renting, and may I add that it couldn't be more chic?

I have not talked about the non-problem girls because to me it's pretty obvious that if you are single, unencumbered by dependents, and financially solvent you are either smart enough to live where you can get to work without a hassle and where you will create the right impression of "style" that is essential, or you are not.

Once settled, you are, I hope, going to want to do a little entertaining, if nothing more than having a few friends over for a drink, and that means the apartment is going to have to look like something. Now, I have written a book on this subject. It's called *Thrift Shop Decorating*, and it is available from my publisher, Arbor House, for a paltry $3.95. However much I would like you to buy that book too, it would be cheating a bit to avoid the issue of what to do with the apartment now that you've finally managed to get into it.

I have an effective solution for sprucing up early attic decor. It's trite, but it works, and it's easy and cheap. (If you have lots of money you don't need me. Call in someone like Mrs. Parrish—Sister Parrish to her inner circle—of the decorating firm of Parrish-Hadley in New York, confide your preferences to her and take a trip to Europe.) Since I'm assuming this is not the happy case, here's the formula: paint the walls a nice dark color like olive green or warm brown, leave the woodwork white if it's notable, ditto the fireplace if you are lucky enough to have one. Dark walls have a way of setting a room apart and making them look dramatic. Now slipcover all of the upholstered furniture in white sailcloth. Do not carpet the floor—in fact, don't rent anything with carpeted floors, not even a garage; with few exceptions carpets are as common as color television. Wax and polish the bare floors—hopefully they are quite dark; if not, stain them and just leave them bare, unless of course you happen to own a really handsome oriental or needlepoint or other beautiful rug. Bare floors are *not* a disaster, they are an asset.

Next, coolly evaluate every ornament, picture, and ashtray you own. Unless you are very discerning, most prints and inexpensive oil paintings are hopeless. Leave the walls bare—since they're dark, they will not seem empty. Remove and discard all decorated lamps, particularly those with silk shades, and replace them with big Chinese ginger jar shapes with pleated white paper shades. Get rid of the tacky ashtrays and buy a few pretty old plates or plain crystal ones. Keep repeating to yourself "less is more."

For table space settle for a generous-size round table (purchased unfinished) and cover it with white sailcloth to the floor. This, plus a couple of sleek Parsons tables (also available unfinished) lacquered shiny black or Chinese red should be enough tables for almost any room. As for curtains, make simple, to-the-floor panels, again of white sailcloth (lined, of course), and wide enough to pull across the windows at night. That's all—if there are venetian blinds, remove them at once and give them to the janitor to store.

Since this is not a decorating book I'm not going on a house tour with you—let me just say that the formula of dark floors, dark walls, and pale fabric uncluttered with junk works every time. And remove the television from the living room—put it in your bedroom or any other place, but get it out of the living room at all costs. This also goes for hi-fi equipment and other such electronic marvels; this stuff should be decently housed in a closet.

Be careful with accessories and plants—if you are not sure about accessories, borrow a few copies of *House and Garden* from the library. Their editorial pages are usually a very good source of ideas.

Chapter Four

Entertaining in Style

*H*aving *fixed up the place,* it's time to go ahead with your plans for entertaining, but go lightly. Quite honestly, it pays to do a bit of observing before you start getting too friendly. I assume your objective is success, otherwise you would not have come this far with me, so at the risk of being called a lot of unpleasant things I earnestly advise you to proceed with caution. I can't tell you who to invite, but a smart girl like you knows where she would like to *be* invited. Therefore, it only makes sense to ask the people whom you would like to have ask you. Pretty simple, really.

Begin your success-oriented entertaining with a few people over for drinks. No matter how many parties you've given in the past or how confident you feel, you have a somewhat different objective now—your party *has* to have style, so start on a scale you can handle comfortably.

The absolutely best cocktail party I ever was lucky enough to go to was given by a very smart and ambitious decorator—believe me, he *had* to have style. Yes, ladies, it was a man, but the plan is easily stolen and I eagerly recommend it to you. There were about eight people on hand. A good-looking black lacquer tray held Scotch, gin, vodka, bourbon and vermouth, with a big silver bowl for ice cubes instead of a tacky ice bucket. That was all except for a pitcher of water and a few bottles of Perrier (naturally carbonated water from France). But on the coffee table was a huge bowl of honest-to-God caviar, with a plate of small rounds of lightly toasted white bread. That was it—no canapes, no olives, nuts, raw vegetables, or dips—just caviar. He could probably have given a dinner for eight for the cost of the caviar, but he couldn't have impressed those people more if he had dancing girls with trays of fruit on their heads. It was a smash.

You do not, however, have to wait until you have the price of a big bowl of caviar. The formula is to have one really great something to eat, not a piddly collection of not-so-hot hors d'oeuvres. A delectable home-baked ham partially carved into small thin slices, the rest left uncarved but accompanied by a razor-sharp knife, can do nicely. All you have to add is a plate of small biscuits or rolls. Put the whole thing on a side table and let people help themselves. Or you can have a big platter of barbecued spareribs cut into bite-size pieces, miniature barbecued chicken legs, or the meaty sections of the wings. Perfect bite-size. You get the idea.

Dinner parties or Sunday lunches take a bit more doing,

but again, if style is your objective the same tactic, "less is more," works equally well. You'll find a group of suggested menus at the back of this book which with the aid of a few good cookbooks should serve you very well.

Here, however, are a few things *not to do*:

Never try to entertain more than four people at a seated dinner party unless you have trained help.

Never serve more than two courses if you are chief cook and bottle washer.

Never have your children at a party; most people, whatever they pretend, are bored by, or resent, other people's children when they go out. Give the kids an early supper, install them in front of their own television, and firmly close the door. If necessary hire a sitter. You owe it to yourself, your guests and—yes—the children themselves. The notable exception to this rule is a party to trim the Christmas tree to which you invite all ages, including other children; just be sure you know who they are and that they can be expected to behave in a reasonably civilized way.

The same goes for dogs. I adore dogs; this book is dedicated to my black Annie, who is part poodle and part what-not. But I have found to my sorrow that not everybody feels the same way, so Annie spends the evening comfortably ensconced on my bed, again with the door firmly closed.

If your mother is living with you, naturally she is going to join any cocktail party or buffet lunch or supper. If it's a seated dinner party and you can handle four, then I think any considerate woman would be reasonably understanding about dining on a tray in her own room. I do know one girl, though, who makes a specialty of only inviting two single men, with her mother making up the foursome. I'll also admit her mother is quite a girl; she usually wears a terrific caftan, lots of pearls, and has her hair done in a brushed-up bouffant "do." The men seem to have a ball; they always accept the invitations, bring the wine, and a fine time is had by all. But that's only one mother.

If you are unsure about table setting—for that matter even if you are sure—check out the rules in any good book on etiquette. Emily Post is the classic, and it's a lot better to be safe than sorry; you might forget something. The party doesn't have to be stuffy, but glaring mistakes like bread and butter plates on a dinner table quickly brand you.

Keep the decoration simple. Fresh flowers (not roses) arranged by you, not a commercial "do," a pretty old tureen, even just a collection of candlesticks (the candles all lighted, of course) make the best dinner party decorations. If you're having a buffet, here the food is really the decoration. Have flowers and candles elsewhere in the room—a buffet table has too much going on already.

Remember, the point of a party is to give people a good time. If they enjoy themselves, they naturally think you are pretty clever, and that's what you had in mind, isn't it? I can't set down any hard and fast rules for you—

there aren't any, to my knowledge—but there are a few essentials that will go a long way toward making any party a success.

Really good food. If you don't know how to cook, buy a good cookbook or two and practice a few "specialties" until you have them down pat.

Good drinks. This means both cocktails and any wines you may be serving. If in doubt, consult the best liquor store in town. Let male guests mix the drinks if possible, it looks better. Have *plenty* of ice.

Have things well organized so that everything goes smoothly.

Make very sure the rooms are neither too hot nor too cold.

Pleasantly lighted, attractive, immaculate surroundings.

Interesting, attractive guests. Cold-blooded as it may seem, never invite dull, mousy people. They are death to any gathering.

Now, all this may provoke some to complain, "Mrs. Williams gives pappy, obvious advice." But I won't cry—I'll just remember that, by God, somebody ought to say it. I've suffered through far too many so-called parties, given by people who should know better, where even the simplest rudiments of successful entertaining were completely ignored. Shall I share some of my memories with you? Well, there was one girl, the wife of a prosperous town official, who staged an Indian porch party. Sounds like fun, doesn't it? It was a nightmare. It was hot as hell, a breathless southern August night, and the porch held only enough chairs and tables to accommodate a handful of the unfortunate guests—the rest had to crowd inside the stifling house. (The air-conditioning was either broken or turned off.) The rooms were garishly lighted by overhead chandeliers (the better to see each other sweat?). By nine o'clock the ice had run out and there was still no sign of food. Finally we were offered our appetizer. This was passed on a tray, and guess what it was? Ice-cold shrimp? No indeedy, it was a mug of steaming hot Indian soup. Clever? Hell, no. There was also no sign of our hostess. A search party finally found her in the kitchen—it was one of those jolly informal parties—chopping onions for the curry that was going to be the star attraction of the evening. It was then after ten, and you *start* making curry by chopping the onions. A group of us slipped out a side door and went home to our air-conditioned house and a supper of scrambled eggs.

And I'll always remember "David." David and his wife were living in Paris, having been sent there by his company, but she had managed to bring the cozy comfort of their Connecticut salt box right into the boissiered walls and thirty-foot ceiling of the 18th-century French town house provided by the company. She had even brought her maple cobbler's bench coffee table and had even removed the gilt-framed mirror over the marble mantelpiece to make room for her collection of real Currier and Ives prints. Well, everybody has a right to decorate her house to suit her fancy, but you don't have the right to inflict bad drinks and bad food on unsuspecting guests. It takes real enterprise to give a bad dinner party in Paris, but David's wife managed it.

David hospitably mixed us a drink as soon as we arrived: "What will it be, Scotch? Bourbon? Vodka?" David had strange ideas on drinks, however; you selected your drink and David would pour a one-ounce jigger of liquor into the bottom of a tall glass, add two ice cubes, then fill the glass with water. The results tasted like the dregs left over from last night's revels. But the worst was yet to come. The little wife had managed to bring some real U.S.A. treats with her—"I just can't eat all this phony French food." We began with "honest" canned mushroom soup. This was followed by fried chicken (she had also brought a can of Crisco shortening), accompanied by mashed potatoes and a lovely gelatin salad made from real lime gelatin, with a timid sprinkling of chopped celery molded into its sicky sweetness. Dessert was a homemade chocolate cake created from a genuine Betty Crocker cake mix.

I'll spare you full-blown accounts of the other horror stories—like driving for half an hour to a luncheon that consisted of a plate of canned soup served with a salad of canned pears, or the cocktail party where the hors d'oeuvres tray was occupied exclusively by a cheese dip and Fritos; or, at the other extreme, the unforgettable Christmas dinner that included roast turkey and dressing, mashed potatoes, baked sweet potatoes with marshmallows (!) on top, canned green beans, canned peas, rice, gravy, canned peaches, gelatin salad, cranberry sauce, applesauce, canned corn, canned asparagus, and three kinds of brown-and-serve rolls that had not been browned enough. There were also three desserts: pecan pie, fruit cake, and ice cream with chocolate sauce. This feast was preceded not by cocktails or a festive glass of champagne, but by eggnog, thick and sweet. Apparently it didn't matter what was served but just that it *was* served.

My point is that it takes thought and care to make a

party go. If you need help, there are quite a few good books on the subject—Dorothy and Mary Rogers' *A Word to the Wives* has fine party chapters; *House and Garden* publishes a good party book; Ceil Dyer has written an excellent book called *The Perfect Dinner Party Cookbook*, with table settings, menus, recipes, wines.

Chapter Five

Keys to Success: Your Manners and Speech

*Y*es, it does help to give a good party. It adds to the image of style you're trying to create and helps to set you apart, just as the right clothes do, and an attractive house and a flair for entertaining do help in the climb to success; they are, more often than you think, a very important factor. Naturally, this doesn't mean you don't have to be bright, competent, and dependable. Of course you do, but an awful lot of B., C. and D. people don't get noticed at all.

Unfortunately even the best house, the best clothes and the best parties are not enough. Now we are coming to the hard part, the part that's hardest to write about and hardest to practice. Women with style are pleasant to have around; they usually are genuinely kind, they rarely gossip, and they *like* to give pleasure to other people. If they are careful about whom they choose as associates and discerning about clothes, houses, and entertaining, they are not being snobbish—life is simply more pleasant that way.

Women who have true style and elegance never borrow—clothes, money, even a cup of sugar. They pay their bills promptly and have the wit and heart to let Amalgamated Department Store wait until the small shopkeeper gets his badly needed check.

They are considerate, not demanding. One of my customers, Jacqueline Onassis, would always preface a purchase by asking in a very soft voice, "Mrs. Williams, could I have that?" Not "Send that to me," but "Could I?" Mrs. Paul Mellon, one of the richest and most attractive women in the world, would ask rather hesitantly if it would be too much trouble to send something to her daughter in Paris—"Would I mind terribly?" Mind? I would have rowed across the Atlantic if necessary. They are unpretentious and polite, notes and telephone calls are answered promptly, and nicest of all, they usually have a good sense of humor.

Finally, the success girls have a common mania for cleanliness and order. Their clothes are always immaculate, their houses shine, and the rooms smell marvelous, a combination of carefully waxed furniture and fresh flowers. Their handbags are impeccable inside and out; their hair may be in the simplest of styles but it is always squeaky clean. They sound awful, don't they? Boringly non-human? They're not, but this is the façade they present to the public. Maybe some of them are first-class bitches on the home front, but you and I will never know, and let me tell you, in business it is so unusual to find any woman who has style, wit, and elegance *plus* ability that she simply has the game all to herself; she can't help succeeding.

I said "finally" to start off the immediately preceding paragraph, didn't I? Well, sorry, but I'm not going to let you off that easily; I still have one more thought on creating a style of your own, so please bear with me just a bit longer.

Here goes: *Don't Put Your Foot in Your Mouth.* Be careful what you say and how you say it. First of all, keep your voice *down*, not to an irritating whisper but low enough so people have to listen to hear what you say. Far too many females have shrill, strident voices. And don't murder the King's English. Find out what words are unforgivable; for help, Emily Post's *Etiquette* and Vogue's *Book of Etiquette* have very good chapters on acceptable usage. Among the inexcusable are "home," when used in place of "house." You can go home, you can come home, you can make your home anywhere you choose, you can be at home, your home can be anything from a trailer to a castle, but you cannot buy or rent a home, only apartments and houses—or campsites, for that matter. A house is a house, you have to make it into a home. Also forbidden are "drapes"—those things at the windows are curtains—and phrases like "pleased to meet you," "T.V." as opposed to television, "phone" instead of telephone, and "classy." It is perfectly okay to be unpretentious; it is only when we try for pseudo-elegance that dry rot sets in. If you are a southerner it's okay to say "Miz" instead of "Mrs." and "supper" in place of "dinner," but don't commit the sin of a fake accent of any kind—English, French, Western, Southern. Fake accents are death. A genuine English, French, Southern, Spanish or whatever accent can be charming; a fake one puts you down as a fool. The worst accent is the supposedly sexy breathless Marilyn Monroe variety; you will not only be considered a damn fool but a bore as well.

You think it doesn't matter? Well, let me give you a small "for instance." I have heard of a very intelligent woman who badly wanted a really good spot that was available with a top flight decorator. She was chic, articulate, had the right background for the job, and all was going splendidly during the interview until the conversation turned to "potios." The interview was quickly brought to a close.

Unpretentious, clear, simple English is the only kind of English to use, and attempts to be elegant by sprinkling your conversation with French or any other foreign words is pedantic and pathetic. Far too many grammatical sins are a direct result of affectation. Don't you be guilty of it. You're too smart.

Chapter Six

Starting Your Own Business

So far, so good. You can and will develop a style of your own that will set you apart from the ordinary and the commonplace, and success does indeed come more easily to the elegant, attractive, pleasant woman; brains alone have never been enough. But what if you really can't find a job in a field that you like and could do well in? Perhaps you have a particular problem that limits you to a dull job. It could be financial responsibilities that make it impossible to start at the bottom (maybe there is no house or car to sell), or perhaps you are middle-aged and have had to face the fact that beginner jobs with any future don't go to middle-aged women (or men either, for that matter). Your particular reason isn't important; what *is* important is to get out of whatever rut you find yourself in and establish a new, interesting, and profitable life-style for yourself.

To start your own business you do need some capital, but probably a lot less than you think, and if you are a fairly capable, responsible individual you can usually acquire the needed wherewithal by taking in a partner. You supply the work, the partner puts up the cash, and you both share equally in the profits after a stipulated salary is paid to you.

Years ago I did the impossible simply because I was too green to know it couldn't be done. I opened a shop in Manhattan on $2,500. The $2,500 was put up by one of the men at an advertising agency where I worked as a part-time fashion director. I had no idea what to sell in the shop; I just thought I would have pretty things for the house.

Well, God looks after fools. After we paid a month's rent and painted the place, the remaining cash was hardly enough to stock a doghouse. We managed to get some merchandise on credit, a few good looking antiques, and a marvelous assortment of baskets was obtained on consignment. It still looked pretty bare, but we hit on the idea of making tablecloths and napkins to order. We had one round table covered with a sample cloth, and had loads of swatches of other fabrics for the customer to choose from. No large inventory necessary. When we made a sale, we would get a deposit. We were very insistent about the deposit (we had to be), and we would then use the money to buy the fabric and make up the order. It worked like a charm. From there it was easy to go on to ruffled pillows, blanket covers and baskets lined in matching fabric to serve as bedside catch-alls. Since this is not a book on how to operate a shop I'll spare you the agonizing details, and simply add that I sold the shop three years later at a very nice profit and opened one in Palm Beach, which I sold two years later at an even nicer profit—and if *I* can do it, any woman can.

Maybe you would hate to run a shop; well, are you a really good cook? Do you have a specialty? One girl in New York made a superlative cheese cake, it *really* was special. She opened a tiny, and I do mean tiny, shop on New York's Upper East Side called "Cheese Cake Unlimited," what else? All she had was cheese cake. But it was all she needed. She had nerve enough to charge an outrageous price, but within two months she was making $500 a week, and the actual baking was being done by two competent women who were delighted with their pleasant work.

My sister makes the most gorgeous cheese spread, a mixture of Vermont cheese, walnuts and cognac. (There's something else in it too, but she won't level with me.) For years she made a pretty good sum out of this stuff, selling it to luxury gourmet shops around New York.

Now I'll be the first to admit that the above case histories could only have happened in New York, Palm Beach, or some other locality where there are plenty of luxury-minded, rich customers who are willing to unbelt to get what they want. It isn't so simple if you live in a conservative community that takes a long look before laying its cash on the line, but it is still perfectly possible to start a business that has more than a passing chance at success.

A friend of mine started a mail order business with

Starting Your Own Business

$200. She began in early summer by running a small but attractive ad on the women's page in a nearby, fairly big-city newspaper. Yes, I know there are no more "women's pages" these days, it's called the "living page" or whatever, but you know what I mean, it's the page where they run the Ann Landers column. Anyway, she advertised a set of three head scarves in pastel checked gingham for $7.50. The first week she received 106 orders. Since she was making a profit of $3.50 on each set, her take for the week was $371.00. Deduct the cost of the ad ($101.00) and the net profit was $270.00. Not bad?

Our enterpreneur continued with one item every week: a long ruffled cocktail apron, also of checked gingham, this time black and white, the whole thing sprinkled with tiny rhinestones (she sold 440 of these); then a log carrier of striped ticking with a bundle of cinnamon sticks for the fire in the side pocket; a man's apron; and so on. She worked out the details with a small local factory to make and ship the things direct, and that left her with not much to do except dream up the items and take the money to the bank.

Back to you good cooks again. If you are really knowledgeable about food, a cooking school can be fun and profitable. It would be tough to start such a school in New York or any other metropolitan city; the competition is too formidable. But in smaller communities you probably have the field all to yourself. A fair price is between $75.00 to $100.00 for ten lessons, two per week. Twenty students at $75 is $1500, pretty good for five weeks' work, even after you deduct the cost of the food for each class. One word of warning here: you have to be good, really *good*, or the whole thing will go sour. This doesn't mean you have to be an expert French chef; you can use your own ethnic background, if you are a marvelous Italian or Chinese cook, for instance. Why not? People love unusual cuisines. Or perhaps you make great pastry and desserts—you can build a school on these alone. What counts is to know what you are doing.

Real estate is another field where women excel. It's easy enough to get a broker's license if you are reasonably intelligent, and believe me, if you are really elegant, chic, and knowledgeable about houses and property you will be so far ahead of the average real estate broker you really can't miss. Two things you must have, though: a lively imagination, so you can make clients see the possibilities inherent in not-so-hot houses, and a good sense of public relations. You are going to have to be well liked so that everyone in town will want to list their property with you and want to buy from you. A talent for entertaining helps (see suggestions in Chapter Four).

The point is to do a little vertical thinking; most people think horizontally only. Let me give you a dandy "for instance."

One woman has hit on a very simple idea. The French are famous for their green salads, correct? No doubt because their salad greens are better. Now, everybody knows the only way to have a really perfect salad is to grow your own greenery. Why not grow French greenery? She now sells six packets of French seeds for salad greens packed in a burlap bag imprinted in green "Le Salade" for $6.00. That's right—*six* dollars. I do not know what she is paying for the seeds, but knowing the French, I can assure you that they would think anyone mad who paid more than a few cents for a packet of seed. Nor is this a pin money business—she sells an average of two hundred bags a week during the spring growing season, which stretches from December in Florida to June in Maine. Let's say she makes only $3 profit on each bag (quite unlikely); even on that small amount the *profit* for seven months is $18,000. Now *that* is vertical thinking. Furthermore, this genius does not pay for advertising, no indeed. The idea is so off-beat that she simply sends a bag of seeds, along with a mimeograph news release, to the biggest newspapers in the country and the editors clamor for the opportunity to run a story. The result is usually at least a half-page article which is absolutely free, not counting the 26 cents she spends for mailing.

The essential point is to market your own talent yourself. Let's say you are good at arranging flowers—you can sell arrangements of silk or dried flowers by mail at a sizable profit. Or you love perfume—charming ribbon-tied bags of homemade potpourri bring a very fancy price. Or you have a gorgeous figure and love to exercise. Start a chic exercise class. Whatever you do, don't just sit there bemoaning your lot. Strike out—you'll have a marvelous time. I have for years.

Chapter Seven

Making It, Keeping It, Enjoying It

When *the man at the bank gets up* to say "good morning," you will have arrived. No, it's not a tribute to your charm; that can help, but bankers usually rise only for well-developed accounts. Success once achieved can be a lovely thing, but don't let it go to your head. And don't assume it's going to last forever—you may well go from strength to strength, but jobs can fold, the economy can fall apart, anything can happen, for better or, equally possible, for worse. That's not being pessimistic, it's just realism.

Now, the usual advice to keep something back for a rainy day, have good health insurance, avoid going into debt, is all fine, perfectly fine, but it's just scratching the surface. The best savings account can run out and hospitalization plans have their limitations; besides, it's rather morbid to plan to be sick, isn't it? And sometime if you're broke you have no alternative but to buy on credit. What really counts in a pinch is your own resourcefulness, and it is far smarter to stay healthy than to allow yourself to slide into sickness. If this sounds self-evident, it apparently is not. I don't know the actual statistics, but it's my bet that at least half the illnesses severe enough to warrant hospitalization could have been prevented by a little sanity. Don't believe it? Look around you. Most people over thirty are overweight, their skins have a gray pallor and a network of wrinkles has set in. They look sick, and will probably get sicker. Hardly surprising in a country where a carbonated, sugary soft drink is the "real thing," and all you fun-loving young people are labelled "the Pepsi Generation," whose diet, according to the television commercials, seems to consist of hot dogs, hamburgers and french fries.

It is cheaper and more fun to stay healthy. You can save an awful lot of money by treating your body with the respect it deserves.

I said resourcefulness counted, didn't I? If you sharpen your wits as you go along and try to keep learning no matter how far up the ladder you have climbed, you need not be thrown by even major setbacks. If this seems vague, let me explain how I climbed out of a first-class mess. I had a really great job in the fashion trade. I went to Europe twice a year (first class, *very* first class), paid for by the company, of course; I had a beautiful office, a secretary, an assistant, and a very substantial salary. To top it off I had a brilliant and compassionate boss. Mac was five years my junior, but we got along like ham and eggs. I really thought I was set for life. I loved the company and the company—a benevolent and solid conservative family business—loved me.

Well, one day the whole beautiful thing exploded in my face. Mac quit. I knew he had had differences of opinion with the super-conservative element, but I had no idea it would come to this. In his place arrived what I considered to be a super-fatted ass. I hated him with an intensity it was impossible to hide. Things went from rotten to intolerable until there was nothing to do but part company; in short, I was fired.

Let me tell you, it was a shattering experience. It took me a few months to recover, but when the money ran out I had to do something. My sister and I set up our own business—a public relations service—she handled food accounts while I specialized in cosmetics and clothes. We did so well that a year after my departure from the dream job I was making double my old salary. I've never been too badly frightened since. The experience taught me that when life hands you a lemon, make lemonade. If you keep learning as you climb and even after you are on top, you will have the resources to make excellent lemonade—even daiquiris, if that's your preference.

The next terribly important thing I'm going to tell you is: *get a good accountant.* It's wise to do this early in your career, but it's absolutely essential if you are making any kind of money at all. A good accountant can save thousands of dollars in taxes, interest fees, bank charges, etc.—all that sort of dry, dusty stuff that accountants seem to love but to my mind and perhaps to yours are a form of civilized torture. What's more, it probably won't cost too much; fees vary according to your needs, but unless you have real problems they are likely to be relatively small.

To find a good accountant, talk to some of your more successful friends; if they are bright enough to make the money, they are bright enough to adhere to it, and you can be sure that means a competent accountant. A last word on the subject: If you are going into business for yourself, hire the accountant before you even hang out the shingle; it's a must.

Now if you hang on to your wit, your health, your resourcefulness and your money, you should be okay; but there's a subtle side to handling success, and it's simply this—*don't take it too hard.* Any successful person, if he's honest, will tell you that there's always an element of luck in making the top rungs—maybe only the luck to be born with a brain that worked in the first place. A lot of people aren't that lucky.

I have also observed time after time that successful women almost unfailingly possess a quality that I can only describe as a joy of life. They are delighted by life, every day is an adventure, they are enthusiastic and optimistic, and they are *aware,* aware of the new and beautiful, of colors and textures, they see beauty as readily in the delicate sheen of a shell as in the luster of real pearls. They are discerning, yes, but only as a means of sorting things out. They are never pretentious.

One final thought: Never, during all my thirty-five years of working, have I ever felt it was a disadvantage to be a woman. In fact, it has always been the other way around, perhaps because I regarded the men I worked with as collaborators, not as competition. (Of course, some of the men made more money than I did, but so did some of the women, and they were frankly worth more.) I believe this was possible because I have always worked in women-oriented fields. I was not competing with men, I was working alongside them, and I never sensed any lack of respect for my competence. This is why I believe so strongly, as I said in the beginning, that women should stick to women-oriented enterprises. Success not only comes more easily, it's *pleasanter*.

It may be terribly old-fashioned, ladies, but the only way a woman is going to get the rewards and respect she deserves is to refuse to cheapen herself, either by the sex kitten approach or by militant feminism. An elegant, intelligent woman of any age can have whatever she wants on her own terms—if she is a lady, not just female.

Chapter Eight

*Escaping from the "American Dream,"
Including the Chrome-plated Nightmare*

*A**re you one of the millions* of women whose suburban life-style has become a cage? If your life is dominated by the supermarket, the children, and the endless round of laundry, housework, and cooking—and you hate it—stop right now and unlock the trap you have set for yourself. Only then can you realize your potential, only then can you succeed as a happy, confident person with your life under your own control again.

Begin with something as simple as finding a grocer and a butcher who will deliver—yes, deliver; they still exist, and with a little searching you can find ones who are reliable and well meaning, and who also have charge accounts. Yes, I know this is flying in the face of every known "new world" economic rule, but hear me out.

Before you place a single order, get dressed—really

dressed, not blue jeans—comb your hair, and personally call on the grocer and the butcher. Explain that you are normally just too busy to come in, that you like to shop by telephone, and while you are prepared to be reasonable you would appreciate a little personal help from them. Now go back home, and the next day telephone in your order. Get organized first, make a list of what you will need that day—no need to buy ahead—and call it in early in the day. From the grocer's point of view you are a dream customer; no fumbling over decisions on the telephone, no long, complicated orders (he's coming by your house the next day too), and no impossible requests. With a charge account, you both benefit. They don't have to collect from you every day, you don't have to write daily checks, and you have a clear record of what you are spending. Pay the bill promptly and it will be one long love affair. One advantage of ordering every day is being able to check what's on hand and make intelligent use of leftovers.

Now you can use the time you formerly spent driving the car to the supermarket, shopping for the food, standing in the checkout line, hauling it home and into the house, for a hot bath, a nap, a game of golf or tennis, a swim, or having your hair done. I guarantee you will be in a far better mood and a lot more charming.

Furthermore, you will save money. It is a proven fact that impulse buying is almost impossible to resist in a supermarket. They are scientifically designed to make you pick up the extra box of cookies, the new detergent, the "specials" that often go unused. By buying only what you really need and want, you will save at least 15% of your current food bill, more than enough to offset the slightly higher prices (sometimes no higher at all) of the service grocer and butcher. That the quality is almost always higher is an extra bonus.

See? You've cut through one of the bars of your cage already. But if you are to break out completely, there's a lot more to it than simply resigning from your job as grocer's delivery boy. You've got to find the time and money to rediscover yourself, to look as attractive and pretty as possible (for your own satisfaction, if nothing else), to have a few luxuries that soothe your soul, to broaden your horizons, and most important of all, to develop your potential as a charming, elegant woman and as a human being, not simply the unpaid laborer that all too many women have become.

Which bring us to the car.

Next to buying a house, the most expensive purchase the average family makes is a car. Now, I'm not against cars; if you simply love to drive and have the leisure and money to afford this expensive luxury, fine, go ahead and enjoy yourself, why not? It's your decision. But *do* you enjoy it? What do you use a car for? For all too many of us the car is used to drive to work (sometimes but not always necessary); drive to the supermarket (*really* unnecessary); drive the children to school, dancing class, scout meeting, ad infinitum, ad nauseam (they would be better off on a bike, and very small children should stay at home); drive to a friend's house for a party (cheaper to take a taxi, safer too, if you plan on imbibing a few drinks); drive to the beach on weekends, a nightmare of heat and traffic; and the ultimate American adventure, drive away on a glorious (?) vacation. My own idea of a vacation is not a cramped car full of fidgeting children who must be endured all day, only to arrive at a plastic motel for the night with the relentless color television set and overcooked hamburgers for dinner.

Maybe you or your husband have no other means of getting to work; in that case, you should seriously consider moving to a spot that's served by public transportation, or better yet, within walking or bicycling distance of the job. If your husband is horror struck at the mere thought of not having a car and you can't convince him otherwise, make it the cheapest one you can get; unless you are super-rich, buy transportation, not chrome. Certainly you don't need two cars.

Now before you start screaming "Without a car I'd be stuck in this house all day and the children would drive me mad," consider this alternative: with just a small part of the money you save on car payments, interest, insurance, gas, oil, tires, repairs and parking you can hire an experienced maid to come two days a week, clean your house, mind the children, and do the laundry. Don't tell me you can't get help, that no one wants to do housework; that isn't true. No one wants to do housework for $2.00 an hour; offer $3.00 an hour. Meanwhile you can get dressed and call a taxi to go shopping, have your hair done, go to exercise class or maybe just have a festive lunch. Two days, six hours a day at $3.00 an hour comes to $36.00 a week, a lot less than the cost of a car.

Stop and think about it. Even cheap cars cost about $4,000, and by the time they are paid for they usually have to be replaced. That's $1,000 a year just for the car! Now you must add insurance, anywhere from $200 to $900 a year depending on where you live, at least another $600 or $700 for gas, oil, tires, repairs and license plates and if you finance the car add at least another thousand; that's $250 more per year! In brief, it's costing you a snappy $2,500 to $3,000 a year for the dubious pleasure of being an unpaid chauffeur. Think what you could do with that money. You could pass up those exhausting excursions to the beach in favor of enjoying your own swimming pool one year, taking a really glorious vacation the next; sock it away for something you really want, use just a fraction of it for some really good clothes, send your kids to college (a poor idea, in my opinion, they should work their way through college)—it's your choice. The point is that you have a choice. It's not mandatory to own a car, even if we have been so brainwashed we really believe it is.

Now what does all of this have to do with being elegant, charming and chic? Simply this: you can't be any of these things without some—not much, but some—time and money, and I think that any woman with the responsibilities of coping with a house and children needs some relief from the endless rounds of cleaning, cooking, and chauffeuring. Reliable help two days a week will give you time for yourself—make the most of it by planning these "mini-vacations."

First things first. If you are not happy with the way you look, take one day for self-improvement. Get to work on your figure; join an exercise class and follow it with a swim, if possible; both are usually available at the local Y, which if not glamorous is certainly cheap, and the effect is the same. After your morning workout have a big salad for lunch, then get your hair and nails done. With help to do the really scrubby jobs around the house, your hands can be pretty and well groomed again.

Take the next day to do something you enjoy, just for the hell of it. Maybe it's touring your favorite museum, or browsing in bookstores, or antique shopping; you name it, it's your day, call a friend and arrange to have lunch together (but stick to the salad routine). I guarantee you will feel a lot more charming, and you will look a great deal better.

On your "vacation" days try to plan something a little festive for your husband too. You'll be in such a good mood that it should be easy to set the table a little bit prettier and serve something he particularly likes. No, it doesn't have to be filet mignon; plain old broiled hamburger will do, but serve it California style on a toasted English muffin and topped with shredded lettuce, grated sharp cheese, and chili sauce. Don't forget to change into something soft and attractive—maybe a caftan that you have made yourself (they are easy)—and light the candles on the table. If your children are small, give them their hamburgers early and pack them off to bed or to watch television while the two of you have a peaceful meal.

Chapter Nine

Liberate Yourself from Consumer Brainwashing

*I*f this book accomplishes nothing else, I hope it will start you questioning a lot of things most people take for granted. The mammoth corporations, with their colossal advertising and public relations budgets, simply put so much pressure on us that we wind up believing whatever we are told to believe and buying whatever we are told to buy like so many wind-up dolls, and no one is more pressured than the young housewife with small children. Saddest of all, she is pressured into believing that hers is the good life. A television commercial may show a pretty young woman carrying an angelic baby while she pushes a supermarket cart which contains, among the children's multi-colored goodies, another angelic-looking child of about three. The girl in the commercial, overjoyed with her lot, happily explains how now all her troubles are over because her new detergent or whatever doesn't require added water softener or whatever. Her hair is glossily beautiful, her nails are impeccable, and she is lightly but carefully made up. Well, I submit that any young woman who has two kids under three and whose entertainment consists of discovering new cleansing materials in the supermarket is not going to feel overjoyed. The truth is, she will undoubtedly look like hell—who wouldn't? She's harassed and tired, both children will undoubtedly be screaming, and the detergent or whatever is probably not going to work a damn bit better than the last one. The tragedy is that too many women are either so defeated they feel guilty about not being happy or so enraged they become avid feminists. Both, I suggest, are wrong. Both have forgotten they have a *right of choice*, a God-given right to make their own decisions.

If, like most of us, you have the sinking feeling that you're losing control over your own life, especially your own money, you are right. You are no doubt buying literally hundreds of dollars worth of stuff you have absolutely no use for, dollars that could go instead for a few really nice clothes (*needs*, not just wants) to keep your self-respect. What is all this money going for?

Well, let's see; I'm not going to try to put this in alphabetical order, but in the order of what products seem to me to be the most useless, but nonetheless the most used:

DEODORANTS AND ANTI-PERSPIRANTS

To me the promotion of these is almost sinful. A healthy person who eats properly does not have an unpleasant odor. Perspiration is fluid normally released by a healthy body. If your diet contains enough fresh fruits and vegetables, particularly greenery, your perspiration will not have any odor at all. Of course, if you don't take a daily bath or your clothes are not washed or cleaned, bacteria from perspiration remaining on your skin will frequently develop and cause an unpleasant odor. So would anything else, if allowed to spoil. I know some of you won't believe me, and after millions of words on television and in print (the question seems always to be not whether to use a deodorant or anti-perspirant, but which one?), who can blame you?

If you want to test my claim, though, I can suggest a simple, cheap routine that should convince you beyond a reasonable doubt. Every day eat at least one cup of minced fresh parsley (this may sound like a lot of parsley but it isn't). Mince up a cupful or two at a time, then sprinkle it generously over everything you eat except dessert. You'll find it adds to just about anything from poached eggs to spaghetti. During the same week swear off all junk foods, pastry, doughnuts, pizza, hot dogs, candy, etc. Instead, eat as much as possible of all the fresh (not frozen, canned, or prepared) foods from this list:

> Apples
> Apricots (dried are okay)
> Asparagus
> Avocados
> Boston lettuce
> Broccoli
> Escarole

Grapefruit
Green beans
Green cabbage
Oranges
Peaches
Pears
Plums
Spinach (preferably raw in a salad)
Tangerines
Watercress
Zucchini

Don't use any anti-perspirants at all during this time. If you do notice any odor during the first couple of days, wipe off your underarms with rubbing alcohol (19¢ a pint as I write this). If at the end of the week you are not absolutely free of any odor from perspiration, you should see a doctor—your system is toxic and you need medical help.

One more word about anti-perspirants: have you ever considered what you are doing to yourself by clogging the pores under your arms with these chemicals? Perspiration is the natural, healthy way for your pores to cleanse the body of impurities. It certainly isn't a good idea to clog them up, is it? And have you read the list of contents on a can of anti-perspirant? As I write this the Federal Food and Drug Administration has just ordered the makers of two leading brands of anti-perspirants to discontinue the use of a key ingredient; it has developed skin cancer in laboratory rats. If you suffer from excess perspiration, it's usually caused by a nervous condition that calls for professional help, but just remember, a little honest sweat is really good for you. Why do you think people spend small fortunes on saunas?

LAXATIVES

I get so mad when I see commercials on television extolling the virtues of laxatives that one day I'm going to throw a blunt instrument at the damn screen, which of course won't do any good at all. I believe that no one—repeat, *no one*—who does not have some problem that ought to be treated by a doctor needs a laxative. Constipation is generally caused by two things: the wrong diet and not enough exercise; laxatives can complicate the problem. I suggest there's a better way. All of the following foods have laxative quailties; any one of them, alone or in pleasing combinations, eaten regularly are healthy antidotes to constipation.

>   Apples
>   Beets
>   Bran
>   Corn
>   Grapefruit juice (freshly squeezed)
>   Plums
>   Prunes
>   Whole Grains
>   Yogurt

One glass of apple juice and one glass of fresh grapefruit juice each day are very effective. In addition, if you have not been exercising regularly, try a few bending and stretching sessions every morning. At the same time cut down on starchy, high-carbohydrate foods. It stands to reason that if you load an already weakened stomach with pastry, french fries, candy, and bread it just gives up. Give it a chance with the right food for a change. Of course, chronic or severe constipation requires a trip to the doctor.

MOUTHWASH

This product has been so blatantly advertised as a cold preventative that the Federal Government has had to step in with a restraining order. However, the damage seems to have been done already, and millions of people dutifully respond like Pavlov's dogs and buy "their" mouthwash regularly. Why are all these products relentless referred to as *your* anti-perspirant, *your* laxative, or *your* mouthwash?—to convince you, I suggest, that there is no question as to whether or not you will buy them, but simply which brand.

Bad breath is caused either by a toxic internal condition and/or bad teeth, and a mouthwash is not a cure for either of these. If you like to rinse out your mouth after brushing your teeth (and you should), plain water is as effective. As for preventing colds or infection, as I said, this claim has been forbidden by law. (Incidentally, if you want to get rid of a pungent odor such as garlic, just eat a few sprigs of parsley—it works beautifully.)

COLD MEDICINE, TABLETS, NASAL SPRAYS, ETC.

The most irritating thing about these products is that the manufacturers assume that you will have a cold. Of course you will, everybody catches cold sometimes, they seem to imply. *No.* Just plain, flat *no.* There is little real excuse for catching a cold unless you are stranded somewhere without citrus fruit. Before you dismiss me as one of those food nuts, let me remind you that you "catch" a cold not because of exposure to cold wet weather or because you were in contact with someone who had a cold; you catch cold because your *resistance* to infection is low. Ample vitamin C will strengthen your resistance, and will actually do more to get you over a cold if you should catch one than a medicine chest full of junk. When was the last time you saw a commercial for fresh citrus fruit juice produced in color and aired at prime time? Not recently I'll bet.

ANTI-ACID PREPARATIONS

I simply hate those commercials—you know, the ones that show the so-called medicine dissolving acid in a glass while the announcer intones "That's just the way Handy Dandy pills work in your stomach." Not in *my* stomach, and I hope not in yours. There is no reason for indigestion or an acid condition unless you have a medical problem that should be treated by a doctor, and you will rarely suffer from either if you are smart enough to eat properly. If you are forced by circumstances to eat a miserable meal and indigestion occurs, a small glass of cold milk will clear up the situation as quickly as the pills. But why eat miserable food in the first place? Even if you have to grab a quick lunch, don't settle for a drugstore sandwich; have scrambled eggs, or a cottage cheese and fruit plate, or buy a piece of cheese, some crackers and a piece of fruit at a grocery store and find a park bench or someplace where you can eat it in reasonable peace.

It's no wonder the peddlers of indigestion "cures" are getting rich. Look at the frightening proliferation of pizza and hamburger chains all across the country, now so successful they can afford prime-time television commercials. I long to tell these hucksters that my way is not to insult my insides with fried meat on a gooey bun accompanied by french-fried potatoes, a cola drink, and apple pie.

I once watched a very fat man in one of these places (What was *I* doing there? Getting change to buy cigarettes) finish off a double hamburger, a large container of french fries and a cola drink; he was in the process of ordering some of the pie. When I asked him for a match, he turned to me and said, "Oh, I don't smoke, it's too dangerous." Now I know smoking is an unhealthy habit to be avoided like any other unpleasant and dangerous habit, but at least the cigarette people are not *allowed* to advertise on television and are forced to provide a warning on their package. If you're still foolish enough to smoke, as I am, at least you are no longer bombarded by hard sell and you are forewarned. I believe there should be equal warnings about bad food; and that dangerously bad food plus any equally dangerous products to overcome the inevitable indigestion should be banned from television completely.

TOOTHPASTE

I'll forgive the toothpaste makers a little bit because their products taste good and they have a nice foamy quality that's sort of fun, but did you know they all contain sugar? Yes, sugar, and unless you rinse your mouth very, very carefully after brushing, you are leaving a coating of sugar on your teeth. Do I need to tell you what sugar does to teeth? Ask any dentist. You can save a considerable piece of change by substituting plain old baking soda for toothpaste. It makes your mouth feel marvelously clean and does a super-job on your teeth. Ironically, a currently popular brand of toothpaste is advertised as containing *real* baking soda! Of course they don't mention the fact that you can get a six-weeks' supply of baking soda for about a quarter.

HOUSEHOLD ODOR KILLERS

Any house that is clean smells good; a dirty house stinks.

"LABOR SAVING" HOUSEHOLD PRODUCTS

Dust-Ending Sprays

This stuff is simply old-fashioned furniture oil in a spray can. If you spray oil on any surface, a mop or rag is naturally going to pick up dust along with the oil. The fact that a film of greasy oil is left on the surface to attract more dirt is ignored.

The reason furniture oil went out of fashion is that back in the days when advertisers didn't promise miracles, the directions on the bottle read "Rub with a clean cloth until thoroughly dry." That was work. I can still remember mama making me rub the O'Cedar polish into the hall table until it was bone dry. Like any sensible woman, she knew that if you didn't, more dirt would collect, then more oil, then more dirt, until you had a greasy scum that could only be removed with lye.

Window and Wall Cleaners that contain real ammonia

The price of these wonders varies from 98¢ to $1.19 a *pint*. You can buy a quart of ammonia for 35¢. A few drops added to warm water cleans as effectively as the "miracle" products. Ridiculous, isn't it?

Drain-opening Preparations

The active ingredient in these products is lye. You can buy the same size can of pure lye at the hardware store for about a fourth of the price of commercial drain openers. Yes, pure lye is dangerous to use; so can be the commercial products, which isn't mentioned in the advertising.

Fabric Softeners and other laundry additives

What's probably making your washables *un*-soft is detergent residue, which can be caused either by using too much of the stuff or by hard water, or both. It's cheaper and easier on your clothes simply to use less detergent, and if the water is very hard throw in a handful of baking soda before starting the machine.

JUNK FOOD

What is the real reason your grocery bill is eating you out of house and home as well as taking the shirt off your back? Food prices are high, no doubt about it, but the truth is, a good fourth of the tab is for non-food products, or foods so low in nutrition, inferior in taste, and expensive that they become rank extravagances. Soft drinks are not only a waste of money but can be a detriment to good health and good looks. High in sugary calories, devoid of any real food value, they deserve to be outlawed. But *you* can outlaw them from *your* budget and *your* body. In warm weather, try making a big pitcher of iced tea with fresh lemon and, if possible, fresh mint. Keep it ready in the refrigerator. Tell the kids it's more grown up than soft drinks. If teen-agers are your problem, sell them on the idea that soft drinks are *corny*.

But soft drinks aren't the only culprits. Prepared salad dressings, sugary cereals, instant potatoes, jams and jellies, hamburger "helpers," stuffing mixes, macaroni "dinners," preparations used to coat chicken (why, God only knows), cake, biscuit and pie mixes (you don't need pie at all), frozen "convenience" foods (the only "convenience" about them is the money they conveniently make for the manufacturer). Add to this list commercial breads, rolls, doughnuts, candy bars, ice cream, so-called cheese "foods" (foods?), chewing gum (this really should be outlawed—a hideous way to ruin your teeth), drink mixes (that are claimed to taste just like fresh fruit—good God!), whipped toppings (have you ever read the list of ingredients?), frozen waffles, pancakes, coffee cakes and Danish pastries (Danish?) ... it goes on endlessly. We can also include such items as paper towels, toilet bowl cleaners, kitchen floor polishes, sprays that are *supposed* to wax your furniture, sprays that are *supposed* to keep food from sticking (ugh!), aluminum foil, plastic wrap, plastic bags, etc., etc.

Listen if you will for a moment—you can keep any house spanking clean with just these following items:

Scouring powder
Ammonia
Baking soda
Detergent
Steel wool (steel wool, not soap pads; buy it at a hardware store for a quarter the price of soap pads)
Dishwasher powder (if you have a dishwasher—I don't)
Paste wax
A bag of old rags
Elbow grease (your own or hired)

Any left-over food can be easily stored in covered plastic or glass refrigerator dishes (a set can be purchased for a couple of dollars), or you can use empty cottage cheese containers—and I hope you buy lots of cottage cheese.

Anything cooked on aluminum foil can be cooked in a pan.

Ordinary dish towels and rags will do every bit as well as paper towels, and since you probably have a washing machine, how much work is it to keep them clean?

If you will confine your grocery list only to those foods and products you really need, you will be astonished at the savings. Learn to plan meals around meat, fish, chicken, eggs and cheese, plus seasonal fresh fruit and vegetables; if this sounds like a lot of trouble, it isn't. In the back of the book I've included menus and recipes stolen from my sister's cookbook file that really work. I've tried every one; they taste good and they are easy, even for me (and I am one of those anti-kitchen cooks who burns boiling water).

Make your own bread, coffee cake, and rolls; it's easy

Liberate Yourself from Consumer Brainwashing   71

and fun; try making bread when you are mad at the world or keyed-up and tense. I guarantee you will feel loads better when you have finished, and with tasteless commercial bread going for over 70¢ a loaf you can't afford not to relax and enjoy yourself by making your own. That the difference in taste between homemade and store-bought is about the same as that between a soft drink and vintage champagne is an extra dividend.

The same holds true for jams, jellies, and preserves. You don't need to make a federal case out of it, but it's almost no effort to make a jar or two of fresh fruit preserves. If you are unsure about sterilizing and sealing, just make small batches and store in the refrigerator. Depending on the season, I make up a few jars of fresh strawberry jam, applesauce, or cranberry sauce every couple of weeks and that's that. And surely you prefer homemade cakes and cookies, and they are simply not that much trouble (please see recipes in back of book).

If all this sounds like near-casual dismissal of a good many very real problems (your kids have tantrums if they can't have soft drinks, your husband complains about lack of snacks in the house, you simply don't have even a few hours for home baking), I still hope you will give the whole notion of cutting down on unnecessary products at least a try. Believe me, it works, and for most of us it's the only practical way to squeeze extra cash out of the budget.

Chapter Ten

Stop Cluttering Your Life with Gadgets

You can save a substantial amount of cash if you forego what I call "adult toys." Perhaps this is a bad name—the only adult thing about them is that they are bought by people over twenty-one —but toys they are and toys they remain. I'm talking about all the totally unnecessary gadgets that an awful lot of grown men and women have been brain-washed into buying. They are nearly always electric—electric skillets, electric can openers, electric slow cookers, electric coffee makers, toasters, etc.; there's even an electric orange juice squeezer that someone must be buying, it is on the market. The fact that an ordinary stove and a supply of relatively inexpensive pots and pans will do the same job doesn't seem to occur. I'll admit that an electric blender and an inexpensive electric beater are handy tools, but the rule of thumb in purchasing any of these play toys should be, "Can I accomplish the same job with what I already have?" Let's take an example. You can't possibly beat up a cake or blend a frozen daiquiri as fast as you can with an electric mixer or blender respectively, and I'll be the first to say that I like a homemade cake and frozen daiquiris; but the truth is, neither one is a necessity—cakes can be made by hand, and the cocktail shaker existed long before the electric blender.

Be that as it may, there simply is no reason for the existence of most of the other gee-gaws. Food cooked in an electric skillet requires just as much watching as in a plain iron skillet on a conventional stove; an electric slow cooker does not impart any more flavor than a heavy stock pot with a close-fitting lid placed over a slow burner; toast can be made just as easily in a conventional oven; and the best coffee in the world is made by pouring freshly boiling water over coffee grounds in a drip pot with a filter—the best of which in my opinion is a simple glass beaker called a Chemex. It's been around for years but it's so simple a lot of people don't take it seriously; it doesn't plug into an electric outlet, so it lacks the glamor of a real all-American toy.

Aren't you a little old to be playing with toys? Wouldn't the money be better spent on buying yourself some free time by hiring help for a few hours, or using these dollars for a pair of elegant shoes or a luxurious winter coat? I believe if you think about it you would really rather have the clothes than the toys, now wouldn't you?

Major appliances like refrigerators and stoves, of

course, are a genuine necessity, but remember—whether you are replacing your old equipment or starting from scratch you are buying a cold chest in which to preserve food and/or a heating element that is going to cook your food. With these essential facts in mind, you will be able to resist the dandy (and expensive) extras that are in fact only toys. An ordinary refrigerator that requires a few minutes to defrost will keep food fresh just as satisfactorily as the glamorous models that fill their own ice trays. Just how much trouble is it to fill an ice tray? A stove with a self-cleaning oven is obviously a blessing, but it need not be pea soup green or bilious yellow and come equipped with a timer and an electric clock. A stove will cook just as well and be even better looking in just plain white than in all the so-called "decorator" colors, which are usually ugly.

What's needed to escape from this nightmare is to shift mental gears into a whole new attitude toward everything in your life. If you are happy with the status quo, who am I to question your life-style. But if you are not, and if you (like many women) secretly or not so secretly long to be elegantly chic, envisioning yourself against a beautiful background where your children are well behaved and meals are nicely served in a pleasant setting, then read on. Most of us would like all these things but we think we lack both the time and the money. But assuming you are not entirely broke, if you have been buying any or all of the things I have mentioned, if time payments on cars, appliances, television sets, etc., are part of your life, then you do indeed have extra money available. You are just spending it on the wrong things.

You *can* change your life, it is simply up to you. You can use your income to buy what you really want, not what you are told to buy; you can control your own household; you can replace disorder and confusion with beauty and serenity.

Chapter Eleven

Are We Becoming a Nation of Slobs?

*T*he *quality needed most of* all, the universal attribute of all successful women, is a zest for life; by that I mean a keen appreciation of all the pleasant things, great and small, which set us apart from animals to the degree that we are civilized. To me, the relatively recent emphasis on the word "casual" has become an excuse to be slobs. It's "casual" to eat in the kitchen, it's "casual" to have our children—and ourselves—appear in ragged blue jeans, their mouths distorted by bubble gum. It's "casual" to have a sloppy house, or go around in badly cut pants in hideous colors, no matter how wide the rear end. Casual, indeed! We are becoming a *nation of slobs.*

Just recently my sister was entertaining the food editor of a large metropolitan daily paper, an educated and supposedly knowledgeable professional person. She was extolling the virtues of her Microwave oven (America's newest toy). "You see," she explained, "I can fix dinner and put everybody's serving in those individual sectional plastic trays. They stack right on top of each other in the refrigerator, you know, then when anyone wants to eat he just puts his tray in the microwave oven and dinner is ready in a few minutes." I had to leave the table. Maybe I'm a voice crying in the wilderness but what *is* this? What happened to the attractively set dining table, lighted by candles, where everyone gathered for a pleasant meal at the end of the day? What kind of people are we bringing up to run the world? I thought sadly of my own childhood, when every day ended with dinner served on pretty plates on fresh linen. There were always flowers and candles, and everyone came to the table neatly—not expensively—dressed and in a pleasant mood. Dinner was the highlight of the day; we looked forward to it. Furthermore, we behaved; sloppy table manners were simply not permitted. No, we were not rich, quite poor in fact; it was just a standard of living we set for ourselves, and we lived up to it. That early good training has given me a lifetime of pleasure. Dinner to me still means a pleasant, nicely served meal, whatever the circumstances.

But how we are pressured nowadays! No one even questions the powers that have thrust this new attitude upon us. If you differ from the norm which some mysterious force has compelled us to accept, you are "peculiar," perhaps even un-American. The other day I read with apprehension a long magazine article about a famous cookbook author whose speciality is fine French food. This person, whose books are nearly as revered as the

Bible, was describing a dream kitchen which included a generous-sized table for dining. There was even a picture of it showing how guests could enjoy their *boeuf bourguignon* with a delightful view of the stove and a sink full of dirty pots. Enchanting, no? The person went on to explain that the house had a dining room but that it was rarely used, and if the person were remodeling or building a new house the dining room would be eliminated. How sad.

One of the unhappy apparent results of this high-touted style of living is the almost complete eclipse of any attempt at table manners. In fact, they don't seem to exist any more for anyone under thirty. Recently I watched two young men in college blazers eating their lunch. Both were well dressed and apparently educated, and both were eating like animals—elbows planted on the table, faces almost in their plates as they shoveled the food into their mouths. After the meal they both brought out toothpicks and commenced practicing dental hygiene. When they were finished they discarded the toothpicks and squashed their cigarettes out in the food remaining on their plates. They seemed unaware of their disgusting performance.

Smaller children? Apparently nobody bothers to teach them. They vie loudly for attention, refuse to eat the meal in front of them and scream for other food that is not on the table. In restaurants they leave the rest of the party before the others have finished to wander about the room screeching out their discoveries or their desires to go to the bathroom. These performances have no discernible effect on the parents, who apparently are cowed by or indifferent to such behavior. Or perhaps they have simply given up.

This passion for "casualness" has spilled over into every facet of life. A well-known decorating magazine, whose excellent articles reflect style and taste, apparently has been forced by economic pressure to accept the advertising of a large furniture company whose copy reads, "You can't change your kids but you can change your furniture." The accompanying photographs show three little unchangeables clambering over some hideous chairs. The copy goes on to explain that even your children can't ruin this stuff. It makes no pretense that the pieces are attractive; the only claim is that they are indestructible. Well, let me tell you, I could change those kids, and I know of no better time for a change than immediately and no better tool than a hairbrush.

Have we taken leave of our sanity? Are we going to permit, indeed encourage, our children to be tyrants? Are children going to be allowed to grow up with no regard whatsoever for attractive surroundings, with no appreciation for beauty, for even the barest essentials of civilization?

Before you can escape your trap and realize your potential as a woman, you have to get control over every aspect of your life that is damaging to your goal, and that includes your children. The irony is that children really want authority; it gives them a much needed sense of security, and sadly enough (for too often they see very little of it), children respond very strongly to beauty, and take pride in a pretty house and an elegant mother. Children love to brag, and will rise to the occasion if given a chance. Try setting the table in the dining room tonight and plan something special on the menu (see suggested "cheap festive dinners" on page 147). Arrange some flowers for a centerpiece. Before dinner is served, change into a pretty at-home skirt or a caftan and ask the kids to clean up a bit; tell them it's sort of a party. In brief, give them something to look up to, to be proud of. If they don't go into shock first, I think you will be amazed at the response.

The same holds true for your house; make it attractive and charming and get them to help you keep it that way. Children love to help, and if you set the standards they will measure up to *your* performance.

Chapter Twelve

An Elegant House:
Order, Simplicity, Color

I'm not amused by the recent proliferation of articles and newspaper columns that tell us how terrific it is to have what amounts to a messy house. We are, I gather, to find it funny when we are told of the torn slipcovers smeared with peanut butter and the closets whose contents spill out onto the floor when the door is opened—and let's not forget those hilarious wads of chewing gum under the dining table. And isn't it a laugh to hear about the author's yellowing philodendron and dying Boston fern? No. Messy, dirty, ugly houses make most people uncomfortable even if they are not aware of it, and certainly you are not going to be very happy yourself in dingy, grimy surroundings. You've got to get your house under control like everything else.

Begin by clearing out. Go through it and discard every

worn, outdated, useless thing you own, from that dinky table in the living room that you hate, to the unused remains of a prescription in the medicine chest. Clean up, clear out, get rid of the junk, take up the worn rugs, throw out the musty curtains, the too-heavy bedspreads, the useless ornaments and gimcracks that are all too easy to accumulate. Wax and polish the floors and furniture with paste wax (you can buy a polisher for about $30.00 or rent one for a couple of dollars a day). When you are through, you'll be amazed at how much better everything looks. Now if you want a complete transformation of your living room, see the decorating suggestions on page 84 and 85.

They offer some workable suggestions that have been successful for me and for a lot of my clients. You'll note that I recommend dark walls and light colored slip covers, but if you hate the idea there's no reason on earth why you can't paint your walls any color you like. Forget all that mumbo-jumbo about cool colors, warm colors, exposure, etc. What matters is that you like it. Just be sure you get a color you *will* like; far too many paint stores insist on selling too pale a shade, and you end up with cream-colored walls when what you had in mind was sunny yellow.

Do please take my advice in the previous chapter and forego carpeted floors; carpets are tacky as well as impossible to clean. Once again, we have been sold a bill of goods. One famous maker of synthetic carpet fibers does not have carpets on *their* floors—that's for us, the poor sheep.

I do want to get very insistent and plead with you not to tart up your house. No curtains at all are better than over-done, elaborate jobs in synthetic replicas of brocade touted as "decorator-styled." Matchstick blinds, in my view, are far preferable to the effect advertised by a mail order chain of stores that offers to make "house calls" and features a delighted housewife seated in front of a window festooned with yards of real imitation brocade complete with tassels, fringe, tie backs, loops, swags, etc. We are told that this may be ordered from home, that they will indeed make house calls. Well, all I can say is the patient died.

Another deadly decorating sin is the use of prints and/or over-elaborate fabrics. Please, I beg of you, *try* slipcovering your upholstered furniture in cotton, sail cloth, or chintz in solid colors—either white or a pretty pale shade. Get rid of the dinky tables and replace them with a fabric-covered round table and the sleek Parsons table previously recommended. Avoid meaningless objects from souvenir or department store gift shops. Confine your ornaments to a few really good things; better yet, if you are unsure, just settle for plain crystal ashtrays, a few handsome books, and baskets of vigorous flowering or foliage plants. Try a tree, a real tree—a ficus is most decorative—in front of the new mercifully freed window. Did you know that when the then Prince of Wales accepted Mrs. Simpson's (later the Duchess of Windsor) invitation to dinner she rented a flowering mimosa tree for her rather bare dining room? She knew what she was doing. Now, there was a real American girl with style.

The keys to an elegant house are order, simplicity, and color. Get and keep your house in order. Systematically weed out old and worn clothing and equipment—this goes for everything from the rusted pie tin in the kitchen to the slightly shabby coat that you hate. Only by constant weeding can you keep the possessions you want in order. If it's too good to throw away, give it away, but do get rid of it.

As for simplicity, I don't think I need belabor the point; when you select a plain lamp with a plain shade instead of a decorated one you've got the message. Buy either the simplest furniture you can find or genuine antiques, and don't you ever be guilty of allowing one of those awful reclining pop-up chairs in your house—it's not a barber shop.

When it comes to decorating, color seems to be the one thing that throws most people. For some reason we have been sold on the mysterious idea that all colors must be "coordinated" and we either run about frantically with swatches trying to match something or other, or just give up on color completely. If you will look to nature for your color schemes you can't miss. Try envisioning some of these combinations: sky blue walls, écru or white slipcovers, dark floors, perhaps an accent piece like a coffee table in lacquer red. Or paint the walls a soft olive green, cover the furniture in pale blue and add a pair of black lacquered chairs with lemon-yellow seats. If you stay with clear, natural colors you can mix them the way nature does with unfailingly pleasing results.

How about replacing those old bedspreads with checked gingham dust ruffles, blanket covers and pillow shams? No, it need not look too frilly for a man; try black and white or brown and white checks. All this stuff is easy to make, and checked gingham is cheap and a snap to care for. It also makes great curtains, just simple to-the-floor panels that can be tied back by day but are wide enough to pull across the windows at night.

I once again remind you to tell yourself "less is more." A bare, beautifully kept wood floor is much better looking than garish carpeting, a bare wall is in better taste than a sleazy oil painting or a meaningless print, a white paper lamp shade is infinitely preferable to a braid-trimmed one of silk. Keep firmly in mind that an orderly clean house even sparingly furnished is far more attractive than any musty, overcrowded place can ever be.

So far I've ignored your children, haven't I? Naturally they have to have a place to play, but that doesn't mean the whole house has to be turned over to them. A room of their own (this is the place for *their* television set) or a garage or basement playroom is a practical necessity, but there is no excuse for the woman who whines, "Well, you know you can't have nice things when you have children." Sorry, dear, but you're just being lazy.

Could I say a word here about noise? Of course normal, healthy children are noisy at times and that's certainly okay, but constant screaming and yelling is not. If your children's raucous behavior gets on your nerves at times, maybe it's because they are being brought up in a raucous atmosphere. Try to keep your own voice down; the sound of elegance is a calm, pleasant voice. Turn down the television and the radio—in fact, turn them off when you are not watching or listening to something special. Try to find quiet times during the day, and have a heart and let your husband enjoy a little peace, too.

You *can* control the noise level in your house, and you certainly should, for it seems there is no limit to what we will inflict upon ourselves, when canned music is piped into literally every enclosed space from supermarkets to dentists' offices. And did you know that ultra-modern dairy farmers pipe canned music into their milking barns? It apparently calms the cows and they give more milk. Obviously that's the thinking behind canned music for us, too.

Chapter Thirteen

Thoughts on Keeping House

I'll admit that I may go to extremes in my passion for cleanliness, but the truth remains that sloppy housekeeping does more to ruin a house than all the decorating sins in the world. And I'll admit that housework can be a bore, but unless you are very rich or live in Portugal or some place where help is inexpensive, you are going either to have to do *some* housework or else live in a mess.

You know that nothing reflects against you as a woman so much as a disorderly house. I'm sorry, but whatever women's lib may say, it just isn't attractive for a woman to be a lousy housekeeper and a bad cook. Please, ladies, don't you realize that womanly charm can get you everything? It's not clever, just stupid, to disdain that old-fashioned expression "womanly charm" in favor of the hard, tough approach or slatternly sex-bitch tactics.

A couple of examples: First, a girl I met a number of years ago in New York. She was hell-bent on a career. Her husband, a science professor at a large university, had pleaded with her to move to the charming university town where they could have a pleasant life with their small son. Instead, she rented a ratty apartment in a bad neighborhood. Every chic career woman lives in New York; at least that was this lady's febrile reasoning. And it seems that she thought the bedroom was the highroad to success, so she had an endless series of not very attractive men trailing in and out of hers, who simply used her as a comfort station. One of them did have the sensitivity to complain that he could not "perform," as he felt uncomfortable with her ten-year-old child in the next room, which was separated from their bouncing bed only by thin sheetrock walls.

She sought my friendship, thinking I could help her in her writing career, and one night I accepted an invitation to dinner. I regretted it immediately—the dingy halls of the building led to an apartment so filthy that the smell literally made one sick. Dinner was canned beef stew which she fondly imagined she had transformed with a cup of cheap wine. There was wine to drink, too, of course; it actually wasn't too bad, either, but who could drink it with the staff that passed as food? She said that she simply couldn't take the time from her "creative" work to learn to cook. The child was mysteriously locked in his room, which she explained by saying he didn't like to sit at the table and would only eat hot dogs with a soft drink anyway. (Who could blame him?) He had also developed a twitch and a phobia about shoe laces—he wouldn't lace his shoes. I left this scene as soon as I decently could, never to return. The last I heard of Edith, her son was in a home for disturbed children and she had been hospitalized for drug addiction. God knows what happened to the husband.

Now let me tell you a far happier story. I've recently met a young woman who is so charming and happy, her presence is like a breath of spring. Her face shows an inner serenity, and her life is so joyous that if one could be jealous of anyone, it would be Elsie. No, she is not rich. She and her husband were teachers, but she stopped working when their child was born to take on the full-time job of bringing up her son and running her household. Her husband still teaches school, and since a teacher's pay is not lavish, they work together as a team. She augments their income by taking on sewing assignments and part-time typing, and baking the most beautiful cakes. They have a charming house, which they work on together, with a big vegetable garden. Elsie is a good cook and puts up a supply of fresh produce every summer. I often wondered what made her such a well-adjusted, happy person and gave her the sane and realistic approach to life which has made her such a lovely young woman. Then I met her mother, a soft-spoken, charming lady who had made a career of bringing up three daughters and caring for an excellent husband. She too had that same serenity, and it was obvious that her children had grown up in an atmosphere of love and security, to become happy women whose sanity and common sense have made a very real contribution to the world. Can you think of a better career? I can't.

Now, I don't think that a clean, pretty house and decent meals are going to solve all the world's problems, but don't you think they would help? And is it such a huge sacrifice to keep a house in good order and learn to cook reasonably civilized food? Housework is not the back-breaking labor it's sometimes made out to be by women's lib propagandists, and let me tell you something else—it can keep you in shape. I love to wax floors and furniture. I daydream along as I do it, and my upper arms at fifty-six are as firm as most women's are at twenty-five.

If you have been guilty of sloppy housekeeping and mediocre cooking, start mending your ways. You will find it rewarding, starting with your own enjoyment, and if you are a young woman pursuing either a career or a husband you can be sure that a well-run house will be an asset to you in either endeavor.

I cannot resist another "for instance" here: a young friend of mine, a tawny-haired, blue-eyed beauty who was complaining to me about the lack of worthwhile men in her life. She knows I have a beau whose generous income is matched by his marvelously kind disposition and mature good looks. "Look at you," she was saying, "you're fifty-six and I'll admit not bad-looking, but what's the fascination?" I replied by asking her if she liked to cook. "Oh, I *hate* it, it's a bore." "Do you like to clean house?" I asked. She looked at me as though I had asked her if she liked boa constrictors. "Clean house! Are you kidding? I'm either going to make enough myself or marry a guy with enough. I don't *ever* plan to do housework."

I tried to explain to her that her lack of interest in creating a pleasant background for living showed through in many ways she might be unaware of. To men, she was a pretty toy, and pretty toys are a dime a dozen. Most men, I told her, liked to come to my house because it was attractive and clean, the food was good and the atmosphere was pleasant. They responded by becoming good friends and making my life more pleasant with invitations, presents, and help whenever I needed it.

I hope I have convinced you. If I have succeeded, you may find the following tip sheet useful for maintaining your well-run house.

Paste wax is invaluable. Lightly applied, allowed to dry and buffed to a soft gleam, it is the perfect finish for all natural wood and painted surfaces. A waxed surface repells dirt and wipes clean with the flick of a dry cloth.

As I've said, avoid carpets—expensive, dirty, hard to maintain. But a waxed floor with area rugs is a snap to keep clean with a daily dry mopping and occasional vacuuming or sweeping. In the summer I use inexpensive raffia rugs, which I simply shake out.

Don't let the brass and silver get ahead of you—polish a few pieces every week so that they're never all dirty at once.

Keep window curtains simple, as I've also said, and forget venetian blinds—impossible to keep clean. Have the kind of curtains that pull across the windows at night for a lovely, cozy feeling.

Don't allow your house to become overrun with bugs. You won't have a problem if you keep every bit of food in tightly covered containers or in the refrigerator. An open box of cereal or crackers or whatever is an invitation to bugs. Clean out the cabinet under your sink frequently—it's a damp place where bugs set up housekeeping if left undisturbed. Leave it open at night to let air and light circulate. If you still simply can't get rid of the nasty creatures, ask your pharmacy for a box of sodium fluoride. It's strong stuff, so handle with care, but a tiny bit placed where it is inaccessible to pets and children will eliminate bugs fast.

Wash out the refrigerator once a week and discard any dreary bits of unusable food. And pull out the refrigerator from the wall at least every two months and clean the floor and walls surrounding it. I guarantee that you will be amazed at what you find back there.

Clean your stove and oven once a week, too. Wipe up spills as you go, but give it a complete going-over once a week.

Whatever you do, every day get the beds made, the dishes washed, the bathrooms neated up, the ash trays cleaned out and the trash disposed of *before* you do anything else. Then, even if you don't have time for major cleaning, your house is in order for the day.

Every room should get a thorough cleaning once a week, but you don't have to do them all in one day, and of course once-a-week cleaning help is a blessing, if you can afford it.

Thoughts on Keeping House

About good food. Here are a few things that work for me:

Always keep a supply of homemade frozen chicken and beef stock on hand for transforming fast cooked foods into dishes that have that inimitable long-cooked flavor.

Know your salad greenery and what to do with it. Select it carefully, rush it home to the sink for a thorough washing, then wrap it in *wet*, clean dish towels. Store it in the refrigerator, where I guarantee it will get beautifully crisp.

Learn how to make your own salad dressing. A simple oil-and-vinegar dressing spiked with a dash of sugar (yes, sugar) is best for green salads. And if you're using mayonnaise, the homemade variety tastes a thousand times better than any commercial brand.

Keep a variety of breads in the freezer, homemade if possible, ready to use in a really good sandwich or to accompany a breakfast or supper dish. Never, never buy, much less eat, that tasteless white sponge stuff.

Learn to put together interesting desserts, imaginative combinations of fresh fruit spiked with a generous lacing of cognac or kirsch. Or unusual frozen combinations like my Rajah pudding, so-called because it is a perfect ending to a curry supper. It's simply a layer of frozen raspberries and a layer of orange sherbet topped by a layer of sour cream lightly sweetened with brown sugar. I freeze this in individual little casseroles, and everyone seems to love it.

The main thing is the *desire* to run a pleasant house, taking pleasure and pride in attractive surroundings and finding enjoyment in entertaining your friends with ease and style. If you have that desire, the rest will be easy; you will naturally have fresh flowers in your rooms, with inviting furniture arrangements, good food and good drink, and I wish you much pleasure in these things. I am sure you will find it, for all it takes is a zest for life and a little guidance.

Chapter Fourteen

Liberation: Having the Best in the Best of All Possible Worlds

There is a world that hasn't bought the "casual" nonsense that we so frequently see prevailing around us. In this country it's often the world of the very rich but not always, and in most parts of Europe it's the everyday world of almost every educated person. It's a world where houses are a refuge from the madding crowd, where there are rooms for peace and privacy, where the so-called "family room" is unknown, where meals are served at a nicely set table, where there is beauty and serenity, where children rise and shake hands when introduced, where they sit like human beings at the restaurant table and eat with some resemblance to humanity. It's also a world where ladies (yes, ladies, not just women) take pride in a well-run house, in their appearance, and most of all in the happiness and success of their husbands. Now, isn't that strange? No, it isn't, for these women are smart enough to know that life is far more pleasant as the charming wife of a successful man than as the shrewish bitch who for some obscure reason resents his ability to provide her with the wherewithal to lead a comfortable existence.

What in the world has all of this got to do with liberating you? Well, I'll tell you. When you start to use your money to buy a little freedom from day-in, day-out drudgery, to buy a better figure and a more attractive hairstyle, when you can look at your hands with pride not embarrassment, when you look about your house and see beauty and order, when your children begin to act civilized and your husband pulls out your chair for you at the dinner table, when you look in your closet and take pleasure in selecting what you are going to wear that day, when you no longer feel tired and harassed, when you have the leisure and money to pursue some activity you enjoy no matter if it's golf or stamp collecting, when you are able to take a glorious real vacation, when you have the money to enjoy a festive meal in a good restaurant, when you can express yourself by using any special talent you may have, you have indeed opened the trap; you are truly liberated, more liberated in my view than any woman with a job which, no matter how pleasant, is eventually tyrannical in itself if there is to be any real degree of success. You have, in fact, arrived at the best of all possible worlds; now you can relax and enjoy it.

I realize that all these pleasant things are not going to happen just because you have given up aluminum foil and anti-perspirants; of course not, but as you gain control over yourself, your children, your budget, and your house, you are also going to help your husband succeed and so reap the pleasure of a larger income and a more comfortable life. It is an absolute cold-blooded fact that an attractive, charming wife who is a good hostess and who runs her house with style and good sense can be the biggest asset any man can have on his climb up the corporate ladder. It's no secret that many companies screen the wife as well as the man for really important jobs. No, this doesn't mean you must play the little housewife following two paces behind the big successful man; it means that the two of you are a team, and frankly, if you are not a team you don't need me, you need a lawyer.

Let's get down to specifics. First, you and your clothes. I have talked about makeup and hairstyles in Chapter Two, and there's an outline on basic clothes there too—actually, chic clothes for an outside job are chic clothes in a home setting as well. Chic is chic. However, you can cut back a bit on street clothes in favor of some really nice lingerie and a lovely morning coat. Add one or two long, pretty at-home skirts or a couple of caftans; both are so easy to make yourself you can afford to splurge a bit on the fabric and wind up with something pretty luxurious.

In fact, why don't you start dressing for dinner *every* night? Don't laugh, I know you have enough to do now, but if you have very small children, have you considered the possibility of giving them an early supper in the kitchen and putting them to bed *before* you change clothes and sit down to have a nice cold pre-dinner martini with your husband? Older children can be happily pressed into service to set the table and do any last-minute kitchen-watching while you dress. Let them join the cocktail hour with sherry on the rocks (this waters it down nicely) or some other mild aperitif. If the thought of serving your children drinks sends you up the wall, relax, a small glass of half sherry or vermouth, half ice water, is not going to hurt any child over eight, and it's a very good idea to start them on the idea of drinking as a civilized social custom, not as a way of getting drunk. I know this all may sound unorthodox and your kids might rather be out playing ball until just before they flop down at the table, but again, you are going to have to try to hold out for civilization: It's bad for anyone, adult or child, to start eating immediately after violent exertion, the body needs to calm down, and besides, sooner or later they are going to have to acquire some minimal social graces and it's never too early to learn a bit of the civilizing process. They will probably love the whole thing.

The basic idea is to break away from the patterns that someone else has set for you. You have a right to cut your own pattern to your life's measurements, whatever that may be. You may well decide that my suggestions sound all wrong for *you*. Fine—I only ask that *you* decide. It is your right—exercise it.

For example, I note with sorrow the emergence of the "family room" in the plans of builders and contractors. That it is cheaper to extend the kitchen and call it a family room rather than include a separate dining room is never mentioned. This puts relentless pressure on a woman who has had a full day of children, cooking and housework; she can't escape from the children until she goes wearily to bed. These rooms are widely touted as the place to watch television, which means you watch only the programs the kids like; there it is again, you are the unwilling captive audience. It is a fact that most modern suburban houses allow little if any privacy, there is little or no place to hide inside or out, and the life-style they have created, with its deadly dependence on a car, is so banal, so devoid of interest that millions of women are literally drowning in a sea of frustration.

However, there's hope for us all. More and more young families are leaving the suburban scene and moving to refurbished older neighborhoods in close proximity to the heart of the city. Wilmington, Delaware; Baltimore, Maryland; Charleston, South Carolina; Savannah, Georgia; Richmond, Virginia; Charlotte, North Carolina and Houston, Texas, are just a few of the cities that have rediscovered their older neighborhoods, with their more spacious houses and comfortable old apartment buildings. Some, like Savannah and Charleston, are restoring a treasury of 18th-century buildings; many others, like Richmond and Charlotte, are renovating late Victorian and turn-of-the-century houses, but all offer a terrific breakthrough after a generation of sprawling suburbs that have spread like a malignant disease over the landscape.

Perhaps this is the move for you. You won't have a family room, thank God, but you will get space to breathe, and you will have a place to hide when you simply can't stand it any more. You will probably have a room that can be used as a library (just imagine, we might bring back reading!), and you will undoubtedly have an extra room that can be used as a children's play and study room. Moreover, you will get high ceilings, fireplaces, and a quality of construction that is unknown today.

Sounds too good to be true? Well, let me give you an example. Recently a women's club in Charlotte, North

Carolina, began a movement to restore an old run-down neighborhood within walking distance of downtown Charlotte. They completely renovated one marvelous Victorian house, sold it at a profit, and began another. The idea caught like wildfire, and today "Fourth Ward," as it is called, is almost completely restored. Most families wound up spending about $40,000 to $45,000 for their houses, complete with renovation. For this, the price of a middle-size suburban nonentity, the purchasers got at least five bedrooms, two or three bathrooms, a living room, dining room, library, pantry, a huge kitchen, four or five working fireplaces, twenty-foot ceilings, solid hardwood parquet floors, a full basement, and a generous porch—sometimes a sun room as well. Added to all this is the freedom to break the yoke of car payments once and for all. Think about it—if you need space and think you can't afford it, it's a wonderful solution. If, however, that much house appalls you, you can often find small carriage houses that can be turned into compact quarters and there are often older apartment buildings that offer spacious rooms and wood-burning fireplaces at moderate rentals.

You can live with a lot more style and chic in the city than you will ever be able to manage in the suburbs. In the first place, the move sets you apart, and that's a step in itself toward acquiring style; second, with space to stash the children away upstairs you can entertain with flair, and creative entertaining is not only fun but one of the best ways I know to broaden your circle of friends and to create an interesting life for both you and your husband, to say nothing of your children.

I've outlined some general entertaining strategy on pages 30 through 37, and of course they hold true for anyone, but thinking you might like a few party plans and menus that have worked well for me, I've included a few suggestions in the last chapter of Menus and Meals.

There's one final point I'd like to get across: get accustomed to luxury. I can hear laughter in the wings on this one, but I mean it. Make your next vacation a trip to Europe and leave the children with your mother or someone else equally or more reliable—they can go when they grow up. Can't afford it? You will be able to if you practice what I've preached to you so far. Make it a brief trip if need be, but stay at a really luxurious hotel for a few days and get accustomed to the food and service that have almost vanished in this country. You will come back refreshed and enriched with ideas for improving your house, your wardrobe, and your cooking skills. If that sounds superficial, it isn't; it's applying civilization to the three basic needs of life—food, clothing, and shelter.

If the budget is really tight, make it a brief trip to Dublin, London, or Madrid; Paris is more expensive, so is Rome. For the money, there's no more elegant hotel in the world than the Russell in Dublin, and it's a fascinating city to explore. In London, plan to stay at Claridge's, or if you prefer a smaller hotel, at the Connaught. In Madrid it's the Ritz. Don't, for God's sake, take any sightseeing buses; do things properly and hire a car and driver; it's not an arm and a leg. Buy a couple of recent guidebooks before you go; the new ones on the market are very good, and there are also excellent restaurant guides that will help you find interesting places to lunch. But if you really want to dine in splendor, dine at the hotel.

Paris, if you can afford it (figure roughly about 35% higher), is of course the most luxurious city on earth. My own favorite hotel is the Plaza Athénée, but the Ritz is pretty splendid too.

Try not to accept the mediocre in any facet of your life. Yes, I know, the best is usually expensive, but not necessarily. It costs more to go out to an ordinary restaurant with its less than ordinary food, taking the children with you, of course, than it does to hire a maid for the afternoon and evening and prepare an elegant little supper for a few friends while she installs the children in their own rooms with their supper on a tray, then helps you serve elegantly.

With just a fraction of the money you save by not buying junk, you can buy some fragrant bath salts and really good soap, plus a dozen or so luxurious towels, to turn your bathroom into a refuge from a hectic day.

Regard perfume as a necessity, but only a good French one, please; buy less expensive cologne if you must, but never cheap perfume. Personally, I think Guerlain makes the best perfume in the world, and there are any number of fragrances to choose from.

Speaking of perfume, it's nice to have a few bowls of sweet-smelling potpourri around the house. You can make your own if you like with dried flower petals and fragrant oils; write to Caswell Massey, Lexington Avenue at 48th Street, New York, for a catalogue of all their fascinating ingredients plus instructions.

Above all, resolve to use your money to buy what you want, not what you are told to buy. The reason nice luxurious things are known to only a handful of the population is that big business wants you, and the small quality manufacturer simply gets lost. Resolve to search for the best, never to settle for second best, and dismiss the hard-sell boys for what they are worth. You may be sure most of them don't use their own products. Just as the DuPonts don't have nylon carpeting, the Wrigleys don't chew gum. I also suspect the largest stockholders in, say, the company that gave us the Pepsi Generation prefer vintage Bordeaux. When Mrs. Merriweather Post had her breakfast brought up by the parlor maid in her forty-room Palm Beach mansion, I wonder if the tray contained Post Toasties, for example.

Don't you think you are as deserving as such people are? I do.

PART TWO
Coming of Age

Chapter Fifteen

The Freedom to Be Yourself

*C*ongratulations—you've made it! You can say good-by to all the fears and frustrations of youth, the insecurity and self-doubts, the dashed ambitions and the daydreams that couldn't possibly come true. The real blessing of maturity is the grown-up realization of what we are and what we *can* achieve. Youth sets impossible goals for remaking the world and shaping it to our own design. The realization that comes with time, that we are probably not going to do much more than make a very small dent, is in a way a relief. Any adult who deserves the name can accept his limitations with a good grace, and this cheerful acceptance brings with it an inner serenity that makes life very much worthwhile. This is not to say that ambition and dreams are turned off at age forty-five, but it does mean, if one truly *is* an adult, that ambitions and dreams are projected toward more possible goals. In short, we know what we can achieve, and the achievement comes that much more easily.

To my mind, maturity especially enriches a woman's life, if she is smart enough to handle it. Gone are childbearing days, and the subsequent nursemaid-charwoman chores—chores that can't be avoided even if a young woman has been clever and bright. Gone is the miserable business of being treated like Miss Sex Kitten, and regarded as peculiar if you don't care for pinches on the bottom from pimply-faced youths and lecherous old men. You can still have all the sex you want, but you can have it on your own terms. Gone too is the hateful necessity of convincing employees and/or customers that you aren't just a pretty little thing with the brain of a pea-hen. Now that you have that greatest of gifts to offer, an adult mind, your opinions are listened to with respect.

Moreover if you are married, you and your husband have probably by this time built at least a reasonably compatible life together; if nothing more, you have learned to live with each other's faults and have achieved a comfortable relationship that is likely to improve with the passing of time. On the other hand, if you are single, widowed, or divorced, you have one of the greatest assets any human being can possess: freedom—and that's no small prize. You are free at last to go your own way, to live where and how you like, to dress, eat, sleep, breathe as you choose.

If all of this is true, why then does one meet so many dreary, defeated middle-aged women? Simply because they have accepted the cult of youth; they believe the propaganda that one must be young at, literally, all costs, and that aging inevitably means deterioration, sickness, ugliness, and pain. Even more haunting is the fear of loneliness, of separation from the world, a fear that becomes a vicious circle as it paralyzes the ability to join the mainstream of life and to enlarge one's horizons instead of constricting them.

What's to be done? First, accept the fact that maturity is a blessing, not a liability. Then set about organizing your life to your own liking, and stop conforming to the preconceived, mindless theory that anyone past forty-five has had it.

First things first: let's be honest and admit that two cardinal sins of age are sloppiness and a tendency to let yourself go. Don't you commit either one. Take yourself firmly in hand; there's no such thing as "middle-aged spread," it's just plain *spread* and would have accumulated at nineteen if you had eaten too much and confined your exercise to getting in and out of a car. If your figure is less than good you have no alternative but to get it in shape. A sloppy figure is just plain ugly, and frankly more "telling" than wrinkles or gray hair. Don't say you can't do it—any woman can have a reasonably trim, lithe body until the end of her days. It just takes a bit of doing. I have personally known dozens of women whose figures were near-perfect at fifty, sixty, or even seventy and over.

The easiest way to give yourself a new body (especially if you do not have an iron will) is to join a health club and, regardless of wind or weather, stick to a routine of at least an hour and a half workout three times a week. Try to find one that has exercise facilities, a whirlpool bath and a steam room as well as a pool. The best routine is a 15-minute exercise workout, followed by ten minutes or so in the whirlpool to stimulate your circulation, then into the steam room for at least ten minutes more, or until you work up a really drenching sweat. After that, a shower to rinse off all the impurities you've just got rid of—rinse your hair too, heads sweat heavily—and wind up with a fifteen- or twenty-minute swim. I guarantee you will feel and look marvelous. Not only will the exercise trim away bulges and droops, firm up your arms and straighten out your posture, but the improved circulation brought about by the entire routine has a fantastic effect on your skin. Your face has a rosy glow that no cosmetic can match, and fine lines and dryness vanish—the moisturizing effect of the steam room is more effective than all the creams and lotions the cosmetic industry can devise. I spent years in the cosmetics industry and I know from experience that you cannot improve your skin by putting stuff on the surface; improvement has to come from within. The dry, gray skin of so many come-of-age women is caused by poor circulation and impurities in the pores, aggravated by lack of exercise and a bad diet.

If you are not knowledgeable about good food at your age you should be embarrassed enough to correct your deficiency immediately. If you like good food, why not invest in a few good cookbooks and seriously go about learning how to cook more sophisticated fare? Now that you no longer have to worry about the "kiddies," their insatiable appetite for hamburgers, and your duty-bound feeling that they must have a good breakfast, you can change over your own eating habits to a more continental style and breakfast on fruit and cheese, with salads and a lovely entrée for luncheon and dinner. Learning to be a creative cook is a rewarding and highly useful avocation. Join a cooking class if you feel unsure of your skills, but one way or another, you should learn. Really great food rewards you doubly in being unfailingly less fattening than those all-American favorites—hamburgers, fried chicken, steak, and pie. If you substitute sweetbreads Marchand de vin for steak, or cold striped bass with sauce verte for a hamburger, or strawberries with kirsch for apple pie, you are not only going to dine well but lose pounds at the same time. The bonus is better skin, clearer eyes, healthier hair and nails.

Brush up on your knowledge of wine at the same time. Good wine not only enhances good food, but by substituting it for hard liquor you are going to cut out a lot of calories. I'm all for a drink before dinner, but the sad truth is that too many drinks are ruinous to a diet, with the added unfortunate effect of making you look bloated —and that is anything but attractive.

The goal of any-age woman should be, in one word, *elegance*. An elegant woman commands respect and admiration.

A woman of any age must also make herself attractive not merely to the opposite sex, but an attractive human being in her own right if she is to achieve a measure of success in any direction. For example, a vital, elegant woman who can give an elegant little dinner party without apparent effort is going to be far more sought-after than the overweight slouch whose only contribution to pleasant living is a querulous whine about "you know how it is when you're older." Learn to cook, learn to play the piano, even badly (people love to gather around a piano and sing), learn to play a good game of bridge, learn how to garden successfully; in short, learn *something* new.

Anyone with a mind at all is often afraid—fear comes in the dark watches of the night, and none of us is immune. To reach beyond our narrow little boundaries is to find freedom, freedom from fear, from boredom, from loneliness. This is the great gift maturity has to offer us, if we will only have the wit to accept it. It doesn't matter what it is that removes us from endless self-contemplation; it need not be helping retarded children to find themselves or teaching Braille to the blind, though both are important and praiseworthy endeavors; it may be nothing more serious than growing prize delphinium or making the best chocolate soufflé in town.

Now if this sounds trivial and frivolous, let me counter with the old cliché that man indeed does not live by bread alone, or even good works, and prize delphinium and perfect chocolate soufflés have their place and serve their purpose. "If you have but two yen," said the Chinese philosopher, "spend one for bread and one for a lotus flower for your soul." And how true this is—if we deny our soul we deny God, we admit to being only animals, unmoved by beauty or by spirit; in fact, we deny our spiritual being, and this is the fate that awaits us if we refuse to acknowledge our *need* for beauty, for serenity.

What counts in this world is not age but that intangible called the zest for life, and it can be as strong at sixty-five as it was at twenty. Zest is the enthusiastic pleasure that we get out of everyday things—experiencing a thrill of excitement at the sight of a wave crashing against a beach, the silent peace of a walk in the woods, the joy of creating anything, whether it is music or great food—the ability, in short, to see beauty and wonder in every moment of our lives. I like to think of a memorable walk in New York that was totally unplanned. I had turned up Sixth Avenue one cold December evening and looked up in the rapidly gathering dusk at one of the towering steel and glass buildings. The sky had turned deep violet blue and all at once the lights in nearly every window went on like diamonds. I made my way home in an aura of happiness created by that electric moment. Silly? I don't think so. I'll always remember those diamond towers gleaming coldly against a velvet sky.

If you have the zest for life I'm talking about, you will want the best there is. You will refuse the shoddy and the cheap, you will have the self-pride that will make you work for a good figure, a well-put-together wardrobe, well-groomed hair and nails. No, not to look younger, but to look your most attractive self for your own sake, as much as for your audience.

Chapter Sixteen

Setting the Stage for a New Life: Your Clothes, Your Looks, Your House

*I*t's hard to be specific about clothes without knowing you. I've tried to give some basic suggestions on page 14 to 15 which apply to *any* adult woman regardless of her age, but there are a few do's and dont's *especially* for any woman over forty-five. Here is a list of do's:

Do wear furs if you can afford them—not a stole but a fluffy collar of pale fox on a sweater or a storm coat can be very attractive.

Do have some glamorous at-home clothes. Caftans are especially easy to make yourself. Try one in hot pink oriental silk, and wear it with strings of pretend rubies and pearls.

Do have some pretty at-home evening shoes. These need not be expensive, but they must be simple; plain silk dyed ruby red can be effective with dozens of colors.

Do wear big, important but simple earrings. One chic woman I know wears huge "diamonds"—no frills, just the stones—with all her evening things; they've become her trademark. By day, try big, thick gold hoops.

Do wear well-cut pants, but only if you have slim hips. They have to fit properly, and they *must* be in a conservative color and fabric, as mentioned before, like beige twill or gray flannel. And always wear them with a well-tailored shirt or a good sweater.

Do invest in quality. You can wear the same clothes for years and still be the chicest woman in town, but shoddy clothes are shoddy clothes even when they're brand new. If you don't have the initial wherewithal, try your damndest to learn to sew. Patterns are much easier these days; in fact, I think Vogue patterns rank with the best designs in ready-to-wear.

Do know your figure and what looks best on you. Take the time to really analyze yourself; now that you are older, thank God, you *can* afford to take the time.

Do indulge in some luxurious lingerie and a pretty dressing gown. If the budget is tight, these are easy to make. I like to use satin de Lys, it's available by the yard in beautiful colors, is easy to wash, and requires no ironing.

And now for a list of *Don'ts*.

Don't, please, ever wear pants suits. I've said this over and over again in this volume, but while they are awful on anyone, they are horrendous on a woman old enough to know better. I don't care who else wears them, *you* are going to look frightful in these garish get-ups.

Don't wear pretty, itsy-bitsy "dainty" clothes, jewelry, or anything else; no, they do not look feminine, just tacky. And never wear white shoes, there is simply no excuse for these monstrosities (see notes on shoes and bags, page 15).

Don't wear hard, garish colors—they are aging—but on the other hand, don't go in for "pretty" pastels—they are pathetic. The chicest colors are beige, gray, camel, brown, black, and true scarlet. A "real" red, very simple evening dress can be a smash, and so is a simple red coat. This rule doesn't apply to at-home clothes, however; there you can go all out for color.

Don't wear over-trimmed "busy" clothes. To be avoided: gilt buttons, braid, top stitching, etc. Even if you can't afford expensive clothes, look at them in shops. You'll find that they are almost always free of such tarty junk.

Now for a word about makeup. I've offered my very opinionated opinions on the subject on pages 11 and 12, but I would like to add one point here that applies to "maturer women": do wear lipstick in a fairly definite shade. But be sure to apply it carefully, preferably with a brush, or it will seep into the skin around your mouth. A crisp clean line is what is wanted, and you can't get it by smearing on lipstick without benefit of a mirror and good strong light.

May I digress for a moment to tell you a true story? My sister and I were driving to Florida one winter in a brand new sports car she had just bought, believing that she was too young at fifty-one to settle for anything more conservative. We were both wearing well-cut pants and cotton shirts. We pulled into a motel for the night, filled the ice bucket, and had just settled down for a drink when the telephone rang and a very young male voice said, "We, uh, saw you coming in just now, we're just across the way, and we, uh, well, we wondered, are you younger girls or older girls?" I managed to explain that we were indeed older girls, and that they would know it if they hadn't seen us only from the back. I haven't gotten over it yet, and the question, "Are you younger girls or older girls?" has become, as you might imagine, a tired but beloved joke in our family.

Well, back to business. One question that comes up frequently with "older girls" is whether or not to have your face lifted. I say, go ahead and do it if you want to and can afford it. It can take a lot of sag and bag off, but what it can't do is make you look twenty-five or thirty again. No way. My sister had a face lift because she was unhappy with what she regarded as a jowly look; she is very pleased with her nice clean jaw line, and is delighted she took the plunge. I, on the other hand, wouldn't have my face lifted if it looked like a map of the Rockies. I'm terrified of the surgeon's knife. If you do it, select your surgeon carefully. Be sure to check with care on his reputation. A word of caution: don't be coy about it—you are not fooling anyone, only yourself. Just tell the truth. "I've just had my face lifted" will disarm the gossipers before they get started.

Successful come-of-age people ought to have a successful house. I've explored decorating pretty thoroughly on pages 82 and 83, and I hope you will take time to read them again. I honestly believe the ideas there are effective in creating good-looking rooms, and they are inexpensive. You'll note I've stressed lack of clutter, which is not just important, it is *mandatory* if you've reached the golden age of reason. Why? Simply because anyone who's been around for forty years or more has accumulated things. What's worse is that all too often the eye becomes so accustomed to the same familiar furniture, bric-a-brac, and junk that after a while we don't see it at all.

I am reminded of a charming couple I know who retired to a golfing resort where they bought an attractive house. These people were not old frumps, far from it; she was slim, chic and attractive, and he had kept his hair, his shape, and his sense of humor. They were well-read, played a good game of golf and bridge; in short; they were fun to know. When they invited me to dinner I looked forward to it with anticipation. Frankly, I was never so shocked in my life—or so disappointed. Their house was one of the dreariest I've ever been in: brown plush sofas facing equally ugly imitation tapestry chairs, a garish reproduction of an oriental rug concealing most of the really lovely floors, tacky lamps topped with fussy, faded silk shades. The dining room was furnished (afflicted) with a mediocre dull mahogany "suite" that vaguely resembled Heppelwhite, and everywhere there was a senseless collection of eyesores picked up God knows where, or accumulated as gifts.

Every decorating mistake imaginable was here, from the fussily over-curtained windows to the metal ash trays in the living room to the cut-glass berry set on the dining room buffet cabinet. I couldn't believe it—how could two such attractive people live with such junk? I finally realized that they were able to because they didn't see it at all. This was the furniture they had been living with for years, transplanted from the city where they had spent the first twenty-five years of their married life. Not good to begin with, it grew less attractive as time went by, but it was so familiar they never thought about it.

I can hear you saying, what difference did it make? They were happy. Isn't that what counts? But, you see, they were not happy, they were lonely. New acquaintances were eagerly asked to cocktails or dinner but the invitations were never returned, and subsequent ones from them were refused. People simply didn't have a good time in that house; the overpowering mustiness and the indifferent food (she was still cooking the way she was taught in her 1939 "home ec" class) just didn't produce much enjoyment. The hard truth is that the world is a hard place; people are not just interested in your heart of gold, they want to enjoy themselves at a party, and if they don't, they don't come back. It's the way things are, and if you can't accept it the only people who will bother with you are the ones who either feel sorry for you or are dreary themselves. Personally, I don't like being pitied—or bored. Do you?

Chapter Seventeen

Money: Saving It, Making More

*N*ow, then. You are chic, elegant, attractive, have a charming house, know how to serve marvelous food, give a good party, are an enthusiastic expert at some interesting avocation. Lovely, isn't it?

Not exactly. It's all very well for me to tell you how to become the sparkling, popular person you have the potential to be, but what if there just isn't any money for clothes (even cleverly sewn at home) or for sprucing up a house at low cost? What do you do when it simply isn't in the exchequer?

There are two answers, neither one of them simple: you are either going to have to make more money or you are going to have to reduce your present expenses. (I said they weren't simple, didn't I?)

Let's take the second answer first, because it's the easier

of the two. I cannot tell you exactly how to cut your expenses because I don't know your precise situation, but here are some general guidelines that could help. First, unless you are tied to a job, consider seriously moving to a different community. If, for instance, you are living in or near a large northern city, you are paying dearly for housing you don't need—higher rent or mortgage payments, enormous fuel bills, higher taxes, higher prices for food, etc. A move to a small town or small city in the mid-South might solve a lot of your problems.

Let me give you an example. I knew a bright, attractive woman of fifty, widowed, with a very limited income; by the time she had paid for a roof over her head and food on the table in a not especially attractive suburb of New York there just wasn't any money left at all. Naturally it's difficult to look great on nothing, and it was difficult for her to replace a dust mop, to say nothing of replacing the slipcovers.

Fortunately, she was a girl of spirit, and after studying some atlases and maps she sent for chamber of commerce literature from the communities she felt would interest her. She wound up in Chapel Hill, North Carolina, the beautiful home of the University of North Carolina, exchanging her $227 mortgage payment for $125 rent on a pretty little Victorian house with two working fireplaces, and reducing her average yearly fuel bill for heat and air conditioning from about $3,000 to about $300. Central heat is needed for only about two and a half months a year in Chapel Hill, and as for air conditioning, that's supplied by nature in a solidly built, high-ceilinged house. Furthermore, as the growing season there is long and productive, she exchanged dubiously fresh supermarket produce at ruinous prices for garden-fresh vegetables at a tenth of the cost. No, she didn't get out the hoe and heave to; for the actual work a local boy was recruited who was happy with a small hourly fee and who also brought fresh eggs and chickens from his mother's farm at prices so low they seemed ridiculous.

Not needing expensive winter coats, boots, and all the other trappings essential in a cold climate meant money was available for a few really attractive clothes, and since the local hair stylist charged exactly half the price of her northern counterpart, it became possible to look well groomed again.

The final bonus was a stimulating community. The university provided access to live theatre, good music, interesting lecture groups and a fine library. Entertaining has become a source of great pleasure, now that she has both people she enjoys being with and the means to do it in style.

If all this sounds just too sugar-sweet, a make-believe happy ending, I assure you it is not. I know because *I* did it, leaving Manhattan after twenty-seven years as a dedicated New Yorker to move to Savannah, Georgia, and I have never regretted it for one moment. The trick, of course, is to find the type of place that suits you. I am passionately interested in restoration so I am in my element in the Historic Savannah Foundation, but if that isn't your cup of tea you would be bored to tears. University towns are usually good bets, offering modest prices (professors are usually not rich) along with a stimulating atmosphere. Or maybe you love horses; the hunt country—Aiken, South Carolina, for example—is a heavenly place to live. Only you can make the decision, but in general, avoid the traditional retirement communities in Florida and Southern California; over-crowding, high prices, shoddy housing and the funereal atmosphere of a community made up almost entirely of retired people are inevitable in these areas.

Moving to a smaller community can also often solve the second problem, how to make more money. It's a lot easier to become a big frog in a little pond, where your talents will be recognized much faster. Of course, if you have been an executive secretary you are certainly going to take a whopping cut in salary, but if you have any training and/or experience in decorating or real estate, it's relatively easy to "break in" in a smaller community, and if you're good, success will come quickly.

If you are married, perhaps you and your husband should consider the idea of a small farm; if you are fond of the country, farm living can be highly enjoyable. The great advantage is that while you can't expect to make a profit from your farm, you can virtually live off the land. I know one couple whose modest retirement income was eaten up by the high cost of bare existence in suburban Chicago. They finally took the plunge, sold their house and furniture, and bought a one hundred-acre farm in southern Ohio. The price was less than they got for the old place, and the farm included a roomy, pleasant house, vintage 1910, whose sturdy construction, pleasing big porch and spacious kitchen made up for the less-than-glamorous single bath.

And they do actually live off the land. A vegetable garden provides more good vegetables than they can eat or preserve, so they built an attractive roadside stand, screened from the house by a grove of tall trees. From the beginning of May until November the stand is manned by the son of a nearby farmer, who works for a percentage of sales. In addition to the home-grown peas, beans, tomatoes, eggplant, squash, corn, melons, blueberries, strawberries and blackberries, there are homemade pies, breads, and cookies, all baked by Martha, the amiable cook-of-all-work, who also does the laundry and cleans the house.

My friends estimate they make about $200 a month profit from the stand, seven months of the year—that's after paying for seed, labor to plant and cultivate the crops, and Martha to do the baking. Their own vegetables and fruit are free; so is their housekeeper. Not bad. This past year they added chickens and a beautiful brown-and-white cow. A nearby spring-fed lake provides fresh-caught fish along with wonderful, safe swimming. Let me tell you, a weekend spent roaming the peaceful countryside, swimming in the lake, and eating meals that include country-fresh eggs and cornbread with real, honest-to-God fresh butter, delicate pan-fried trout with just-picked corn and sliced ripe tomatoes, followed by fresh blackberry pie with a scoop of hand-churned ice-cream made with real cream can ruin you for life—you simply never want to go home.

Moreover, they had the sense to furnish the house with a touch of wit: the porch is filled with old wicker furniture painted white and fitted out with sky-blue pillows, a Victorian "parlor set" upholstered in a cabbage-rose chintz graces the living room, while the library is a most comfortable refuge with its deep leather sofa and yards of books you've always wanted to read. The dining room has a round oak pedestal table lacquered white, with a side table that holds a collection of prize pink geraniums in a flat basket. Upstairs, it's all gingham check and brass beds, and while there is only one bath, it is lavishly comfortable with a huge tub and stacks of fluffy white towels.

Did I say they were happy? Do I need to? Oh, yes, I forgot—the electric bill has disappeared. The house has no electricity; lighting is provided by kerosene lamps and candles. Cooking is done on a stove fed by butane gas, which also powers the water heater, while refrigeration is supplied by a huge, old-fashioned ice box, now thoroughly refinished in shiny white, that holds a one hundred-pound block of ice replenished every three days by the ice truck from the nearby town. If you are old enough, one taste of ice tea made with old-fashioned ice will bring back a flood of memories of how good ice used to be before it began to taste vaguely of whatever had been stored alongside it in the refrigerator.

But let us assume that for one reason or another you can't pull up stakes, or that even if you do, there still is not enough money to live the way you would like. You simply have to earn enough to bring your budget into line. Start by sitting down and making a list of your abilities and accomplishments; write down everything, even if you think it has no commercial value. Are you well read, knowledgeable about literature? Or about music? Are you experienced at running a household? Do you give good parties? Are you an expert cook? Are you good with plants and flowers? Do you have great taste and an eye for color and furniture? Perhaps you like people and love houses? Any one of these can provide a substantial auxiliary income. I know one woman whose passion is reading; she conducts two "Great Literature" classes a week for teen-agers from September to May. Students sign up for the term but pay a flat fee of $35 a month. She accepts a maximum of ten students each season, and there is a waiting list. That's $350 a month for a total of three hours' work each week. Of course, she has to bone up on her reading constantly, but she loves it. One note of caution: as with all successful endeavors, she really has something to offer; she knows her subject and enjoys sharing her knowledge. Don't plunge into a venture like this unless you've got the background for it.

As I mentioned earlier, real estate and decorating offer many possibilities to the mature woman, for here age is an especial asset, certainly not a liability. In most states a two- or three-year apprenticeship is necessary before you can obtain a broker's license, but most real estate offices are happy to welcome a knowledgeable, mature woman to their staff on a commission basis. I've already completed my first year as an apprentice, and my commissions have netted me about $9,000 this past twelve months; even more important, I love selling houses, and my time is my own. I've mentioned real estate as a profession in a previous chapter, but to my mind, this is such a good way to earn money it's worth repeating.

As for decorating, you can't just hang out a shingle without training, but most decorating firms are *looking* for a mature, tactful woman whose good taste and color sense can be used to soothe temperamental clients. If this interests you, look around. Don't expect big pay, but you can usually earn a pleasant $90 to $100 a week for a relatively easy job—a very good supplement to a small fixed income.

A friend of mine was complaining about the terrible

manners of most children when I asked her, "Why don't you do something about it?" Believe it or not, she did—she started an etiquette class for teen-agers. Frankly I had my doubts, but the venture is a roaring success. She is a model of social graces herself, and she has a wonderfully warm, persuasive personality. She has that bunch of former roughnecks actually enjoying learning how to behave in a reasonably civilized way. She charges $50 for eight two-hour sessions twice a week, limiting the group to twenty—that's $1,000 a month.

Explore the possibilities. You can teach other women how to give a good party, if that's your speciality, or how to cook. You can buy a small greenhouse, on time if necessary, and put your green thumb to work growing flowers and plants which will net you a nifty sum. There are dozens of ways to add to your income easily and pleasantly—you have only to open your eyes to your own talents.

Chapter Eighteen

Man Talk

And now, ladies, we come to a huge problem that I have carefully swept under the rug until this moment. Let's bring it out in the open: *You're single and you don't like it.* It's that simple. Some women *prefer* to remain single—I for one do, though I'm not saying that someday I might not change my mind—but for many women being single means not being very happy; they are used to male companionship, and they prefer to have it through marriage. I like it too; God knows I don't want to give up men, even for Lent, but I've grown spoiled and selfish in my old age and prefer my own ways, as many single women do, and that's no foundation for a happy marriage. But let's say you *do* want to get married—who am I to tell you how to do it when I'm single myself? Well, I'm single through choice. I've had three respectable offers of marriage in the last three years, and I am at fifty-six no glamor queen. So, for the price of your rapt attention I'll once again mount my soapbox and do what I love most—give advice.

Rule number one (and absolutely essential): *Live alone.* Surely your children are grown up by now, and as much as you love your sister, brother, mother, or Cousin Mary, let them live in their houses and you in yours. It dosen't matter if it's only a one-room apartment. The only possible exception to this rule is your responsibility to aging or ill relatives, particularly your parents. No woman can be called attractive who has openly walked out on a helpless relative; it makes her appear heartless and mean, which indeed she is. Did you ever meet a man who wanted a heartless bitch for a wife?

Learn to distinguish between what a man looks for in a wife and what he looks for when he simply wants to have a good time. Unless you are a fool, the man you want will probably be as old as you are, if not older, and few mature men, unless *they* are fools, want to risk the ridicule of their friends and associates by marrying a cute little Miss Sex-Pot. He can have an affair with her and he'll be regarded as quite a boy, but marry her? That's another story.

Most reasonably intelligent, mature men are not looking for a romance. They want a pleasant companion who is fun to be around and who is elegant, witty, and attractive—someone who can make *their* lives more pleasant. Although it should be obvious to anyone who has had sense enough to reach the age of forty-five without making a complete fool of herself, some women seem unaware that nothing drives a man away faster than pursuit. Despite the brave new world of women's lib, most men still like to do their own hunting, and if a man is old enough to attract you, he probably doesn't buy the brave new world idea anyway. Nor does it do any good to pursue some sport or hobby that really doesn't interest you, with the thought of meeting a man. Go in for any activity that is of genuine interest, with your sole objective enjoyment and perhaps the opportunity of learning more about it for its own sake, and you will meet people you will enjoy—naturally.

Which brings me to another point: regard men as people (a surprising number of women do not), simply people, some charming and intelligent, some bores, some stupid or inane—the funny mix of the human race all over the world. One of the nice things that happens when you simply relax and go about your own life is that you accumulate a lot of men *friends*. There's nothing more enjoyable for a single woman than a group of dependable men friends. I couldn't live without mine.

Let me give you one of my "for instances." I once lived for six months in an apartment complex that consisted of a group of small townhouses clustered around a single courtyard. Unfortunately, I had installed the telephone on a counter in the kitchen just opposite the window facing the courtyard, and could not help observing two of my neighbors' comings and goings. (I am constantly on the telephone, either selling a house or talking to friends.) I almost became a real nosy parker—I moved away just in time. But that's not my point here. The two neighbors were single middle-aged women, one a tall, chic creature who always looked marvelous, was constantly off on some trip or other, and obviously led a happy, active life. The other woman was equally good-looking, but her relentless pursuit of men was embarrassing. She apparently had decided the way to meet a man was to play golf, and she relentlessly played golf (very badly) in fair weather and foul, attaching herself to any group of men unfortunate enough to be on the scene. Afterward she would sit around the club lounge trying to strike up a conversation with any male she could snag. How she could fail to realize that she was being carefully avoided, I will never know. But this was not her only mistake. One day my essential telephone suffered a fit of the vapors. I rang her bell to inquire if I could use her phone to call the repair service. She cordially ushered me into the living room and produced the telephone from its hiding place, a rather ornate box. After I recovered from that one and had succeeded in getting Ma Bell to agree to send the emergency squad, I looked around the room with astonishment so intense it must have been obvious. I hadn't seen a room like this since a 1940 movie. It was decorated like the parlor of a bordello. Silk curtains were drawn across the sliding glass doors that I knew led to the apartment's only pleasant feature, a small garden; the resultant gloom was lightened only by lamps shrouded in silk shades and fitted out with pink light bulbs, the very French furniture was covered in pale blue silk, and a "love seat" (what else?) was cozily drawn up to the fireplace, fitted out with pale rose silk pillows. There was even a fussy coffee table holding a cut-glass decanter of some liqueur and just two (of course just two) glasses. The last straw was the supposedly sexy fragrance that emanated from a lighted candle and the strain of soft music wafting from some unseen source. That kind of setting might light the amorous fires in a man if she had been a twenty-five year old sex queen clad only in a satin dressing gown and her shoulder-length mane of thick red hair; as a background for a fiftyish woman whose face was a bit parched from the golf course and whose costume consisted of a golf skirt and a cotton T-shirt, it was ludicrous. Any man would take to the hills.

Her mistake was to believe that the grand passion was *all* life had to offer, and to cling desperately to that illusion.

Now, you can look at that two ways: you can mourn your lost youth and fool yourself that if you try hard enough you can recapture the old appeal; or you can regard it, as I do, with an enormous sigh of relief. The truth is, most middle-aged women don't *really* want the mad passionate affair. Time does take its toll, and M.P.A.'s are exhausting. What most women do want, if they have any brains at all, is a man in their life, a nice comfortable man who will provide love, affection, and companionship. Someone to share a pleasant life, to enjoy being with, to banish loneliness and the fear of being alone. And that is what most middle-aged men want too.

Now for the end of my story. Neighbor number one met a terrific guy at a seminar on antique china—she was an enthusiastic and knowledgeable collector and so, it turned out, was he (a lot of men are interested in the arts, too, you know). They were married shortly thereafter and promptly bought a house big enough to hold their joint collection. I sometimes see neighbor two at the club, still pursuing, and alone.

You are far more likely to find the man you want if your own life is a happy one, if your house is pretty, pleasant and homelike, with fires burning cheerfully in the winter and a fresh, airy feeling in the spring and summer. A big, comfortable sofa and a well-stocked bar are considerably more alluring to a man old enough to want to relax and enjoy life than any amount of so-called "sexy" decorating. What's more, corny as it may sound, good food is a terrific attraction to any man. No, not necessarily the obvious roast beef or steak, but just really well-cooked, interesting food served with style. In short, if you are pleasant to be around, the hours spent around you are pleasant and interesting and you won't have any trouble finding a man; men will find you, you'll be able to pick and choose, and that is a fact that any woman can prove to herself.

A word of advice that I hope isn't necessary: Don't be mean. I can just hear you—"mean! I'm never mean." Maybe not, but most people are, at least occasionally; not deliberately, perhaps, but mean, nevertheless, and it does scare a man off! I'm talking about the meanness of not paying small creditors promptly, of overworking and/ or underpaying anyone who works for you, of being able to pass a beggar by, of ignoring the misery of a frightened, lost, or injured animal, of callously locking a pet in an airless car, of not seeing the longing on a kid's face in the ice-cream store, of carrying tales or even casual gossip, of taking up a helpless sales person's time when you have no intention of buying, of belittling anyone, friend or foe or family. No woman is attractive if she lacks compassion; she isn't a real woman, for a woman who lacks sympathy and innate kindness is no bargain for anyone. And you know something, you can't hide it. You can be just adorable as long as he's around, but any man will know if it's just an act; I'm sorry, but it shows in your eyes.

Chapter Nineteen

Europe on Nothing a Day

One way to meet people (meaning men) that works every time: travel. Yes, I know it costs money, but if you are ingenious you can often get the trip at least partially paid for, and sometimes you can arrange things so you can go for nothing at all. I have one word of caution so important that if you disregard it, you may as well stay home. Travel *alone*. I don't care if your dear friend Eloise or Eleanor or Susie or whoever is dying to go with you and you can split the expense and have a marvelous time exploring Paris together—*don't*, even if you lose the friendship. Two single women haven't got a Chinaman's chance of meeting anyone but another single woman. It's funny, but a lot of women don't seem to realize that men can be shy too, and two women can seem rather formidable.

On to brighter things; the way to get your trip paid for is to offer a service someone would like to buy. I went to Paris every summer for years by offering to cover the Paris collections for a women's news syndicate. I did the job for $500, which was a lot cheaper than they could get a professional journalist to do it, and while it did not pay for the entire trip, it was a big help. It was also a lot of fun getting a chance to see the famous designers and their clothes. I did have a good background in fashion, and that helped, but anyone with clothes sense and a little writing ability could do the same. You might work out the same arrangement with your local newspaper if it's big enough to pay something but not big enough to send its own women's editor. One year I got four medium-size papers to do it, and that paid for the whole trip.

But fashion reporting is not the only way to free-load your way around the world. My sister has made five lavish trips to Europe and one to Mexico without spending a dime. She offered to write a foreign food column for the local newspaper, then contacted the public relations department of the country she was planning to visit. They were usually only too eager to pay for the trip. That may sound far-fetched, but it worked. She gave them good value—a series of articles which helped to increase tourist interest. She does know a lot about food, I'll admit, but so do many other women who don't do anything with their talent.

Writing isn't the only way to pay for a luxurious trip. I have a friend who takes a group of four teen-agers to Europe every summer. Never more than four, and the kids are an asset, not a liability, to her social life. Somehow a woman seems more attractive having a good time with a bunch of young people than she would alone. Naturally you have to be responsible and conscientious and your first objective must be a successful trip for your charges, but that's fun, not hard work. You also need to know something about the places you are going to visit, but a thorough and intelligent studying up on your itinerary beforehand should satisfy that requirement.

Europe need not be your only destination; it's fairly easy to sell a travel article on any interesting place, and you can escort teen-age kids on other junkets as well. Stay away from New York, Washington, Boston and Los Angeles in the summer months, though; they're all hotter than hell's fire and anyone with any sense tries to leave town.

Or you might sell a shopping service to help pay for your trip. A surprising number of people want things not available in this country, and are happy to pay a reasonable fee to someone who will bring them back. A friend of mine pays for her whole trip to England and France every year this way. Here's how she does it. About the first of May she places a small ad in the newspaper offering to shop for anything and everything as long as it's legal in both countries. She has never failed to get a substantial response. She also sends a very simple sort of newsletter to her previous clients asking if they need something this year. Her fee is 20% of the purchase price, and believe me, it's worth it. I always get her to bring me back some very special candies, perfume, and a few jersey shirts in a certain style that I've been wearing for years, all from Paris and unavailable here. The $50 fee is well spent. She has become such an expert shopper that she is now bringing back samples of new things she finds in her travels, and her orders are bigger than ever.

Chapter Twenty

Husband-hunting? Relax and Enjoy It

I know, all this is just lovely, you get free trips, but what you are looking for is a husband. Well, you may or may not find him. Everything in this life is a gamble, and you will enrich your own life with travel whether you come back with a man or not. Here, however, are a few tips that will help you achieve your goal; they have worked for me in my innocent quest for men friends, and for my serious husband-hunting friends.

Stay at the best possible hotels. That quaint, musty little "find" on the Left Bank in Paris is going to attract only quaint, musty people, and unless you are a glutton for punishment you don't want that kind of man in your life. Stay a shorter time if need be, but the best hotel in town is also the best for your purposes. The kind of man any sensible woman wants is essentially a practical soul who likes the comfort and pleasure a good hotel affords. Don't, however, be taken in and check in at an expensive but dull place; investigate first, know what you are paying your hard-earned dollars for. As I've said, in Paris *the* hotel, in my opinion, is the Plaza Athénée (right across the street from Dior), in Madrid it's the Ritz and in London the Connaught or Claridge's. (See page 136 to 137 for a few more tips on travel.)

The same rule holds for all your travelling. Go first-class, or don't go. In general, save your money and don't go by air; airplane trips are too brief to allow any friendships to develop, and the brutal truth is that most people, men and women alike, are so nervous aboard an airplane that they can only get high on the free liquor. If you don't believe me, find out the hard way.

Having spent many miserable hours watching most of my fellow passengers get mildly drunk, I reached a final decision not to squander any more money on first-class air travel after a recent trip to Paris. Aboard our first-class section was a well-known actor. His companion was a paunchy middle-aged man who, I was to find out, was the senior vice-president of a large soft drink company. They didn't have soft drinks on that flight; they got roaring drunk and spent the entire night chasing the stewardesses and slapping the other passengers on the back, accompanying themselves by singing loudly and out of key. All objections to their behavior were met with, "Aw, c'mon, let's have some fun, c'mon, what'sa matter, what'sa matter with ya?" I like a good time, but being cooped up with two sloppy drunks is not my idea of fun.

I suppose the airline thought they were too important to cut off their liquor supply. It was very unpleasant.

Train travel, to my mind, is the best way to go anywhere. I have met dozens of interesting men on trains, including John Pope-Henessey, the author of Queen Mary's biography, who proved to be one of the most interesting people I have ever known. In general, European trains are superior—for real luxury, take the Blue Train from Paris to Nice—but there are still some great trains here and in Canada. One of my favorites is the Metroliner from Washington to New York.

In general, if you are a charming, attractive, truly mature woman, you aren't going to have any trouble finding friends of both sexes—they will find *you*, so just relax and enjoy yourself.

Now let's assume for a moment that you are *not* looking for a husband, that you have a perfectly good one you are quite happy with and have no desire to turn in for a new model. Well, if you do, and you would like to keep him, may I suggest that you overlook his occasional falls from grace? I don't mean just flirting with another woman—that's never serious, though some misguided women tend to make a federal case out of it—but a real out-and-out affair can be shattering. The worst reaction you can have is over-reaction. Forget the tearful accusations, the divorce threats, the hysterics and histrionics. In a word, cool it and wait. More often than not, the whole thing simmers down and the lamb returns to the pasture grateful that you haven't blown the whole thing apart.

It's bad when a woman cannot accept the fact that

almost all men stray from the fold occasionally; many a hasty divorce has been repented at leisure. European women tend to be more realistic than Americans because they haven't been sold that childish dream that once married they are forever entitled to a life of perfect bliss. We're like children—when we don't get what we want, we have tantrums. Marriage is not and never can be one long happy dream; it takes some work and a lot of sense to keep even a good marriage strong, so if your man is worth it to you then why not try to let the storm blow over? Storms always do; the amount of damage they leave behind depends on how smart you were about protecting your holdings.

Chapter Twenty-One

You're Old Enough to Know Better

I have but one more sermon on the pitfalls and pleasures of middle-age or older, and in a nutshell it is this: you are old enough to know better. Know *what* better? Well, to recapitulate, you are old enough *not* to buy junk food, not to be taken in by the hard sell, not to buy useless and sometimes even dangerous products (for some thoughts on these see pages 59 to 66), *not* to accept senseless slavery to the automobile, *not* to spend good money on electric toys. (See pages 72 to 75), to know better than to neglect your teeth or to allow your body to degenerate into overweight flab, or to let your mind rust from lack of use, or to be poisoned by meanness, greed, gossip, or jealousy. You do indeed know better than to settle for anything less than your true potential. Decide for yourself how you want to live and spend your money, don't let it be decided for you by the hucksters.

You are also old enough to remember a lot of good things that are fast vanishing because a whole generation has grown up unaware of pleasures and luxuries that were once taken for granted. These are the men and women who have never ridden a really luxurious train and who blindly accept the deterioration of our railroads and the tyranny of the automobile and the airplane, blissfully unaware that the malignant alliance of the highway construction industry, the oil interests, and the automobile makers have maneuvered us into a position where we must buy their products. The same people think that over-crowded air terminals and stifling cabins where people are packed six across, exactly like sardines, is the only way to travel any distance, the sole alternative being of course the car. They are unaware that first-class long-distance travel used to mean an immaculate pullman car attended by a smiling white-jacketed porter, and that dinner was not a plastic tray filled with lukewarm defrosted food but an elegantly served meal that might include broiled brook trout and hot blueberry muffins for breakfast, and filet mignon with Bordelaise sauce for dinner.

This is a generation that (with few exceptions) has never enjoyed a luxurious hotel; its idea of a good hotel tends to be a color television set and a dial-it-yourself telephone in every room. We passively accept the plastic food and lack of service as part of the natural order, never questioning the fact that big business has taken over the hotels too, and the computer, not the chef, is in charge of the dining facilities.

We do not question the moral or legal right of giant food and beverage concerns to hard sell food that is at worst harmful and dangerous, or at best so low in nutritional value and honest taste that it is a wasteful extravagance. Nor do we question the right of big chain supermarkets to give so little space and/or attention to fresh food. We accept plastic-wrapped produce that may have stood for hours, if not days, under fluorescent lights, thereby robbing it of food value, and plastic-wrapped meat, cut with an eye to the largest profit, not the most nutrition. (Marrow bones, a cheap source of high protein, are just about not available at all.)

What can you do about all this? You can protest intelligently. You can patronize what's left of the good hotels and the good trains; you can turn your back on the supermarket in favor of the few independent grocers still around; you can refuse to buy junk food. But you can do still more—pick your passion and try to get others to join with you. I belong to a club of railroad buffs who are actively fighting to restore at least some semblance of first-class service. Maybe we won't succeed, but at least it's better to try than simply to accept the indignities forced on us by the total indifference of big business to any other pursuit than a fast buck. And if we can show them that good service means more profit, even they may see the light.

Don't, however, succumb to the temptation to mourn the good old days; fight, yes, but the lugubrious lament "things aren't like they used to be" is futile and boring, to say nothing of aging you faster than anything else under the sun.

How far down the garden path have we come? A long way from the unpaid chauffeur, house cleaner, and children's servant, have we not? At least I hope you have come along with me, and that you have broken out or are now better equipped to break out of your own trap. You can do it, you know, for though these are only words on paper they are real ideas that work. They have worked for me and for a great many women I know—happy, good-looking, vital women who have discovered that indeed a self-serving brain is a far more effective tool for liberation than a crowbar. Well, I hope you are on your way. Good luck—you deserve it!

Chapter Twenty-Two

Menus and Recipes

*H*ere are some of my favorite recipes. I hope you will enjoy them. This is, of course, a book on how to live well, not a cookbook, but I'm sure you'll agree that good food is an essential part of good living.

SEATED DINNER

Oysters on the Half Shell
Choice of Hot (or not
so Fiery) Cocktail Sauces

Thin Sliced Mild Rye Bread,
lightly spread with Sweet Butter
(Cut bread in half or into "fingers")

Champagne

Braised Fillet of Beef*
Parslied New Potatoes
The best (Red) Bordeaux you
can find (and afford)
This course to be followed by
(never serve it with)
Tossed Green Salad
Camembert Wedges
Thin Sliced French Bread

Dessert

Fresh Strawberries
Grand Marnier Sauce
Filtered Coffee

Very Fine Imported Swiss
or Italian
Miniature Chocolates

Cognac

Braised Fillet of Beef

¼ pound salt pork
1 four- to five-pound fillet of beef
2 tablespoons butter
½ cup chopped celery
½ cup chopped shallots
¼ pound chopped mushrooms
1 cup dry red wine
Beef stock
Salt
Pepper

* Asterisks after certain dishes indicate that the recipe will follow the menu.

Wash salt from pork and cut it into small dice. Place in a large, heavy pot over medium heat, and cook, stirring often, until all the fat has been rendered. Remove and discard pork dice. Heat fat until it is almost smoking. Add fillet of beef and cook, turning occasionally, until well browned on all sides. Remove meat. Pour off and discard fat, add butter to pot. When melted (low heat), add vegetables, and cook until soft, stirring often (about ten minutes). Place meat over vegetables and pour in wine, then add sufficient stock to bring the liquid half way up the sides of the meat. Cover and braise for about ten minutes to the pound. Remove meat to serving platter and set aside. Strain cooking liquid and return it to the pot. Cook over high heat until reduced by about half. Season to taste with salt and pepper.

Slice meat and pour some of the sauce over the slices. Serve remaining sauce separately.

Serves eight to ten.

ANOTHER SEATED DINNER
(equally good but not so depleting to the checkbook)

Gazpacho Salad*

Baked Chicken with Sherry-Peach Sauce*
(A low-calorie dish, very chic)
Rice (wild, if you want to splurge)
A Dry White Wine
Pineapple Sherbet with a bit of
Liqueur poured over

Coffee

Gazpacho Salad

- 3 cups tomato juice
- 1 bay leaf
- 2 cloves garlic, peeled and split
- 1 thick slice lemon
- 1 tablespoon lemon juice
- 3 peppercorns
- 1 teaspoon sugar
- 2 envelopes unflavored gelatin, softened in ½ cup cold water
- ½ cup chopped celery
- ¼ cup chopped green pepper
- ½ cup peeled and chopped tart, crisp apple

Combine the first seven ingredients in a sauce pan and let simmer over low heat for about fifteen minutes. Mixture will reduce by about one-half cup liquid. Remove from heat and strain into a second pot. Bring almost to a full boil, remove from heat, and stir in softened gelatin. Cool. Then chill until mixture begins to thicken, and add chopped celery, green pepper, and apple. Pour into six half-cup molds and chill until firm.

To unmold quickly: dip each mold briefly into hot water, then loosen sides with a silver knife. Invert onto serving plate and tap lightly, and the salad will slide out easily.

Serves six.

Baked Chicken with Sherry-Peach Sauce

- 1 three to three and one-half pound chicken, cut into 8 serving pieces (remove and discard backbone)
- 1 cup chicken stock
- 1 cup fresh ripe peaches, peeled and chopped
- ½ cup dry sherry
- Salt and pepper to taste
- 1 tablespoon arrowroot, mixed to a paste with about 1 tablespoon water (optional)

Preheat oven to 350 degrees F.

Place chicken pieces in a single layer in a long, shallow baking dish. Bake in preheated oven for thirty minutes. Remove each piece from baking dish and blot off excess fat. Pour off and discard fat in baking dish and wipe it clean with paper towelling. Return chicken pieces to baking dish and set aside.

Combine stock, peaches and sherry in a sauce pan. Bring to a boil, then lower the heat and let simmer for about ten minutes. Pour into container of electric blender and blend until smooth, or cook mixture until peaches are soft enough to mash with a fork, and mixture can be blended to a purée. Season lightly with salt and pepper.

Pour over chicken in baking dish. Return dish to oven and bake a final twenty to twenty-five minutes.

Arrange chicken on serving plate. If desired, thicken sauce with arrowroot paste.

Pour sauce over chicken and serve at once.

Four servings.

DINNER PARTY FOR A SUMMER NIGHT

Broccoli Vinaigrette
Sweetbreads Marchand de Vin
Wild Rice
Cabernet Sauvignon
Brandied Bing Cherries over
Vanilla Ice Cream
Coffee

SUNDAY LUNCH

Cold Striped Bass
Sauce Verte
French Potato Salad with Watercress
Chilled Dry White Wine
or
Pale Ale
Hot Orange Soufflé
Coffee with Cognac

LATE INFORMAL SUPPER

Plenty of
La Jolla Fish Stew*
Hard Rolls
Beer or White Wine
Deep Dish Apple Pie*
(served still warm from the
oven) with wedges of
Cheddar Cheese
Coffee

EASY AND QUICK SUPPER

Italian Beef with Zucchini*
with plenty of
Freshly Grated Parmesan Cheese
Crusty Italian Bread
Red Chianti
(or an inexpensive California Red Wine)
Fresh Pears or Apples
Bel Paese Cheese
Coffee

La Jolla Fish Stew

2 tablespoons corn or safflower oil
2 tablespoons butter
1 clove garlic, peeled and minced
1 small onion, peeled and minced
2 teaspoons curry powder
1 cup dry white wine
1 one-pound can stewed tomatoes
1 cup water
¼ cup brandy
3 pounds fillet of flounder, whiting, or bass—
    or 1 pound of each
1 pound uncooked shrimp, peeled and deveined
1 pound fresh or frozen crab claws (optional)
Salt and pepper to taste
Crusty French bread (preferably one day old)

Heat oil with butter in a stew pot, add garlic and onion, and sauté until limp. Stir in curry powder. Add wine, tomatoes, water and brandy. Bring to a boil, then lower heat and let simmer for about fifteen minutes. Add fish, shrimp, and crab claws. Cook until fish is white and firm. Season to taste with salt and pepper.

Serve from the pot, or transfer to a heated tureen and ladle over slices of bread in large soup bowls.

Serves eight or more.

Deep-Dish Apple Pie

- 2 frozen patty shells (from Pepperidge Farms, package of 6)
- 5 to 6 cups peeled, cored and chopped crisp, tart apples
- ¾ cup white or light brown sugar
- 2 tablespoons lemon juice
- 2 tablespoons quick-cooking tapioca
- 2 tablespoons butter

Preheat oven to 350 degrees F.

Thaw patty shells until soft but still cold.

Combine apples, sugar, lemon juice, and tapioca in a bowl and let stand about thirty minutes. Transfer to a well-buttered baking dish, dot with butter, and bake in preheated oven for thirty minutes, or until tender.

Roll out thawed pastry. Cut into squares, then cut each square into three or four strips.

Remove apples from oven. Increase oven heat to 425 degrees F. Arrange pastry strips over apples. Return dish to oven and bake until pastry is puffed and lightly browned, about ten minutes.

Italian Beef with Zucchini

1 tablespoon butter
1 tablespoon oil
1 pound top round beef, ground
1 large onion, peeled and chopped
4 medium-sized zucchini, thinly sliced
1 large tomato, chopped
Salt
Freshly ground black pepper
Grated Parmesan cheese

Melt butter with oil in a large skillet. Add beef, and sauté until no longer pink. Add onion and continue to cook, stirring, until limp. Add zucchini slices and chopped tomato. Stir to blend. Cover and let simmer until zucchini is tender. Season with salt and pepper. Serve each portion generously sprinkled with Parmesan cheese.

Four to six servings.

EASY BUFFET PARTY MENUS

With drinks in the Living Room: Paté Maison*

On the buffet table: Chicken Curry with Rice and Accompaniments*

Pale Ale, a good imported brand

For dessert: Rajah Pudding

Coffee

Paté Maison

Mix equal parts butter at room temperature with top-quality liverwurst, add brandy (or Cognac, if you're rich) with a bit of abandon, flavor to a nicety with Escoffier (brand) Sauce Diable, salt and freshly ground black java pepper, and mix well. Heap into a serving bowl and refrigerate until flavors mellow and blend and the paté is firm.

Chicken Curry

    4 tablespoons butter
    1 cup peeled, cored and finely minced tart apples
    ¼ cup finely minced onion
    2 tablespoons flour
    2 tablespoons curry powder (a top-quality brand)
    ½ cup dry white wine
    2 cups clear, fat-free chicken stock
    3 cups boned and skinned poached chicken,
        but in large chunks
    ½ cup sour cream
    Salt to taste
    Cooked white rice
    Minced parsley
    Chopped dry roasted peanuts
    Raisins (plumped in a bit of brandy)
    Minced green onion

Melt three tablespoons of the butter in a large, heavy skillet. Add apple and onion and cook, stirring over very low heat until very soft (about one-half hour). Add remaining butter. When melted, stir in flour and curry powder, blend well and add wine and chicken stock. Let simmer over very low heat until apple is reduced to a pulp and sauce is thick and smooth. Add chicken and sour cream. Season to taste with salt. Stir until heated.

Serve over just cooked, hot, fluffy white rice. Pass minced parsley, chopped peanuts, raisins, and minced green onion to sprinkle over each serving.

DINNER A DEUX

Easy, very Elegant

Sliced Tomatoes Vinaigrette
Skillet Beef with Beans*
(*A reverse-snobbish name for
Tournedos & Flageolets*)
Cabernet Sauvignon
Cheese and Fresh Fruit
with Crusty Rolls
or serve instead
Fresh Fruit Tarts (*from a good bakery*)
Coffee (*demi-tasse, of course*)

Skillet Beef with Beans

- 1 tablespoon oil
- 1 tablespoon butter
- 4 fillets of beef, each about ½-inch thick
- 1 one-pound can imported flageolets (white beans)
- ¼ cup (bottled) Escoffier Sauce Diable
- 1 tablespoon Worcestershire Sauce
- Salt
- Freshly ground black pepper
- ½ cup minced parsley

Heat oil with butter in an electric skillet. In it quickly sear fillets on both sides, then cook to desired degree of doneness (rare is best). Add beans, Sauce Diable, Worcestershire Sauce, season with salt and pepper, add parsley. Stir to blend. Cover and cook until beans are heated.

Two servings.

A CHILDREN'S PARTY

A Du Pont Recipe

Hot Buttered Popcorn
Peanut Butter and Jelly Sandwiches
Lemonade
Brownies, Vanilla Ice Cream
Birthday Cake (from bakery)

Kids like simple fare—Mrs. D. says this is *always* a successful combination of favorite foods.

A GOURMET PICNIC

Shrimp Salad
Cold Lemon Baked Chicken
Thin Bread, Butter and Watercress Sandwiches
Muenster Cheese
Fresh Pears
Dry White Wine

OTHER EASY MENUS

A Super Salad
Hot Rolls
Iced Tea
Old-Fashioned Strawberry Shortcake
(I always add Coffee)

Potage St. Germain
French Bread
White Wine
Fresh Fruit Bowl (any fruit in season, with a bit of Kirsch)

Homemade Cookies (from the freezer)

Coffee

BUDGET MEALS

SUPPER WITH AN ITALIAN ACCENT

Frittata (Italian Potato-Cheese Omelet) *
Spinach Salad with raw sliced mushrooms
Crusty French Bread
Currant Jelly—Sweet Butter
Jug of Wine
(My choice: Almaden Mountain Red)

SHOW OFF YOUR EXPERTISE— COOK-AT-THE-TABLE-FOR-COMPANY DINNER

Dried Beef (the poor man's Prosciutto wrapped around Thin Wedges of Melon)
Fettucine Alfredo*
Italian Bread
Sweet Butter
Soave
(or inexpensive California White Wine)
Amaretti
(Italian Macaroons—you'll find them in some supermarkets, otherwise an Italian grocery)

Frittata

1 tablespoon mild oil
1 tablespoon butter
1 cup diced cold boiled potatoes
¼ cup minced green onion
¾ cup cooked green peas
5 eggs
1 tablespoon grated Parmesan cheese
Salt
Freshly ground black pepper

Preheat broiler to high.

Heat oil with butter in a large (ten-inch) heavy skillet over medium heat. Add potatoes and onions and stir-fry until potatoes are flecked with brown and onions are limp. Add peas and cook a half-minute longer.

Beat eggs with cheese until blended. Season judiciously with salt and pepper. Pour mixture over potatoes and vegetables and cook *without* stirring until eggs are set on bottom of pan. (I repeat, *don't stir*.) Transfer skillet to preheated broiler and cook until eggs are puffed and set.

Cut into wedges to serve.

Four to six servings.

Fettucini Alfredo

2 tablespoons butter
½ cup heavy cream
¼ cup grated Parmesan cheese
Salt
½ cup minced parsley
1 one-pound package flat noodles
1 teaspoon oil
¼ teaspoon salt

Bring butter and cream to room temperature.

Arrange 1 tablespoon butter, the cream, grated cheese, salt (just bring in the shaker) and parsley in attractive plates or bowls on a tray and bring it to the serving table. Set table with warm serving plates.

Cook pasta with oil and salt in a large pot of boiling water. Drain into a colander when tender, but *not* overcooked ("al dente" is the term, meaning no starchy taste but still just faintly firm to the bite). Return cooked pasta to the still hot pot, add the second tablespoon of room-temperature butter, and toss quickly. Bring to the serving table. Add butter and cream, sprinkle lightly with salt. Add parsley, toss quickly again and serve at once.

Four to six servings.

ANOTHER EASY, DO-IT-ALL-AHEAD MENU

*Chinese Roast Fillet of Pork**
*Oriental Rice**
*Stir-Fry Vegetables**
Beer
(*the best imported brand*)
Kumquats and Fresh Pineapple Cubes
Almond Cookies
Fortune Cookies

Tea, if you must, but I always serve coffee too.

Chinese Roast Fillets of Pork

- 2 whole fillets of pork, about 1 pound each
- 1 one-pound can Chinese plum sauce (available in Oriental grocery stores)
- ¼ cup soy sauce

Bring pork to room temperature. Heat oven to 400 degrees F. Place pork in a shallow baking dish in preheated oven. Roast for thirty minutes. Reduce oven temperature to 300 degrees.

Combine plum sauce and soy sauce, pour over meat. Cover baking dish and seal with foil. Continue to bake for another forty-five minutes. Drain, saving sauce. Slice meat. Cover with a little of the sauce. Serve remaining sauce separately.

Six to eight servings.

Oriental Rice

Put cold, boiled rice in a long, shallow baking dish—one-half cup per serving will do nicely. Add chopped waterchestnuts, two or three for each half cup of rice, and raisins (about one tablespoon for each one-half cup rice). Sprinkle soy sauce over all, enough to color but not soak rice. Toss with fork. Bake uncovered in 350 degrees F. oven until heated through. Toss again, and serve.

Stir-Fry Vegetables

- 1 tablespoon butter
- ¼ minced green onion
- ½ cup sliced celery
- 1 ten-pound package frozen mixed Chinese vegetables, with sauce cubes
- ¼ cup water
- 1 cup shredded lettuce
- Soy sauce

Melt butter in a large (ten-inch) skillet. Add celery and onion. Cook, stirring, until vegetables are limp. Add frozen vegetables and water. Stir until sauce cubes are melted, and vegetables can be separated. Cover and steam for about four minutes. Add lettuce and stir to blend. Season with soy sauce and cook, stirring, until lettuce is limp but still green.

Four to six servings.

SUNDAY BRUNCH

(This never fails to please)
Champagne and Fresh Orange Juice (half & half)
or
Whiskey Sours
*Corned Beef Hash
with Eggs**
Hashed Brown Potatoes*
Broiled Fresh Peach Halves
Heated Rolls
Strawberry Jam
Sweet Butter
Lots of really great Coffee
Miniature Danish Pastries

Corned Beef Hash with Eggs

¼ cup finely minced onion
¼ cup finely minced green pepper
2 tablespoons butter
1 teaspoon mild oil
2 one-pound cans corned beef hash (buy the best brand available)
2 tablespoons Escoffier Sauce Diable (or, if you must, substitute 1 tablespoon steak sauce)
Dash Tabasco Sauce
Salt
Freshly ground black pepper
6 large eggs

In a large skillet sauté onions and green pepper in one tablespoon of the butter and all of the oil until very tender. Add corned beef hash and second tablespoon of butter. Break up hash with the tip of a spatula and cook, stirring often, until heated. Stir in Escoffier Sauce (or steak sauce) and Tabasco sauce. Season with salt and pepper. Continue to cook and stir for five to ten minutes. Transfer mixture to a long, shallow baking dish (or individual oval baking dishes). (Can be made ahead up to this point.) Ten to fifteen minutes before meal is to be served, make six shallow indentations in the hash with the back of a tablespoon and break an egg into each.

Cover baking dish or dishes tightly with foil and seal. Place in the preheated 375 degrees F. oven and bake until egg whites have set and yolks are as firm as you like them, about ten to twelve minutes.

Serves six.

Hashed Brown Potatoes

5 medium-size California "white" potatoes
2 tablespoons vegetable shortening
Salt
Freshly ground black pepper
2 tablespoons melted butter

Bake potatoes several hours, preferably one day ahead.

Refrigerate until very cold. Peel and grate on the coarse side of a hand grater.

Heat the shortening in a heavy skillet. Add potatoes (do not pack down). Sprinkle lightly with salt and pepper. Pour melted butter over surface. Cook over low heat until lightly browned on bottom.

Place pan under medium-high broiler heat and cook until surface of potatoes is lightly browned. Turn out onto round platter, cut into wedges to serve.

Serves six.